D1564008

GARLAND STUDIES IN

THE HISTORY OF AMERICAN LABOR

edited by

STUART BRUCHEY
ALLAN NEVINS PROFESSOR EMERITUS
COLUMBIA UNIVERSITY

A GARLAND SERIES

UNDEREMPLOYMENT AMONG ASIANS IN THE UNITED STATES

ASIAN INDIAN, FILIPINO, AND VIETNAMESE WORKERS

ANNA B. MADAMBA

GARLAND PUBLISHING, INC.
A MEMBER OF THE TAYLOR & FRANCIS GROUP
NEW YORK & LONDON / 1998

Library of Congress Cataloging-in-Publication Data

Madamba, Anna B., 1965–
    Unemployment among Asians in the United States : Asian
Indian, Filipino, and Vietnamese workers / Anna Madamba.
        p.   cm. — (Garland studies in the history of American
labor)
    Revision of the author's thesis (Ph.D.)—Pennsylvania State
University, 1994.
    Includes bibliographical references and index.
    ISBN 0-8153-3006-5 (alk. paper)
    1. Underemployment—United States. 2. Asian Americans—
Employment—United States. I. Title. II. Series.
HD5709.2.U6M33 1998
331.6'25'073—dc21
                                                    98-15137

Printed on acid-free, 250-year-life paper
Manufactured in the United States of America

To my family

Dad and Mom, Jeanette and Patrick,
Joey, Tina and Matt, and Lucas

Contents

List of Tables

List of Figures

Foreword

On the eve of the twenty-first century, few political issues are as salient to the future of the United States as immigration and global economic competitiveness. The current policy debates on immigration primarily focus on restricting the number of illegal immigrants and on increasing the human capital of legal immigrants. The policy debates on global economic competitiveness often focus on jobs and international trade issues. Largely absent from this debate is an important concern which links immigration and economic competitiveness—use of immigrant workers in the United States economy is linked not only to immigration policies restricting low-skilled immigrant workers, but also to labor force policies that seek to reduce labor underutilization and mismatches of more highly skilled immigrant workers.

This book brings a unique perspective to the intersection of immigration and labor force competitiveness issues. Building on the shoulders of the pioneering work of such labor force demographers as Clifford C. Clogg, Philip Hauser, and Teresa Sullivan, this research applies the Labor Force Utilization Framework (later known as the Labor Utilization Framework or LUF) to the experience of Asian-American workers in the United States. A premise of this research is that the commonly used unemployment statistic is not an adequate indicator of the economic performance of Asian workers in the United States labor market and therefore does not provide adequate information for labor force policy. What is needed, it is argued, is an understanding of *under*employment, to describe adequately the quality and quantity of work provided by the labor force for economically active immigrant workers.

Dr. Madamba's innovative study focuses on measuring and explaining not one but four forms of underemployment. To my knowledge this book is the first to apply the Labor Force Utilization Framework to the economic assimilation of Asian American workers.

The standard *underemployment* measure—economically active persons without employment as a percentage of the total labor force—is one workable description of labor utilization. However, another closely associated form of underemployment is *involuntary part-time employment*—persons who, although at work, are working less than full-time because of economic reasons. In another form of underemployment, some workers are working full-time, and hence counted as adequately employed by the standard labor force participation method, but their wages are near or below the poverty level. These workers are *underemployed by low income*. A final form of underemployment is especially relevant to the experience of some Asian workers in the U. S. economy. They are fully employed in regard to time spent at work, but are inadequately employed because their skill attainment (educational level) is considerably greater than the skill requirements of their jobs. These workers are defined as *mismatched* in this study.

Dr. Madamba skillfully uses 1980 and 1990 U.S. Bureau of the Census Public Use Microdata to assess underemployment patterns for Indians, Filipinos, and Vietnamese compared to white workers in the United States. The large sample size and the high quality of these data permit an unusually rich and statistically robust analysis of the four forms of underemployment for men and women workers. A key finding is that all Asian worker groups had higher underemployment rates in 1980 and 1990 than white workers in the United States. The descriptive patterns also showed a decrease in unemployment, working poverty, and job mismatch but an increase in part-time employment for recent years for these Asian workers. For all Asian American groups and both years, total women's underemployment was higher than men's. Statistical modeling showed that Asian-American workers' human capital, labor force economic sector, and immigrant assimilation indicators help explain the patterns of national origin and gender differences in the underemployment of Asian workers.

In this era of an unusually high number of total immigrants and even historically high Asian immigration to the United States, this book documenting the inadequate use of Asian workers in the U. S. economy is not only timely but central to this country's labor force policy considerations for the twenty-first century.

Gordon F. De Jong
Distinguished Professor of Sociology
Population Research Institute
Pennsylvania State University
University Park, Pennsylvania

Preface

In spite of the typical picture of disadvantage that accompanies the study of minority and immigrant groups, Asians in the United States have seemed to emerge from this typecasting virtually unscathed. With their generally higher educational achievements, Asians have had greater success at placement in more preferable occupations in the labor market. This later translates into greater economic success compared to the typical immigrant. As such, the stereotype of the Asian as the "model minority" was proposed.

My interest in labor migration and immigration has motivated me to study this group that seems to be set apart economically from other immigrant groups. Experience and anecdotal accounts tell me that the model minority stereotype does not exactly hold true. While complete integration in the labor market is not yet a reality and Asians do have difficulties there, they do suffer some economic hardships, and these economic experiences vary across Asian ethnic groups. A number of research studies have substantiated this claim. Therefore, in an effort to try to explain the Asian employment experience, I hypothesized that because of the higher educational background that Asians take with them into the labor market, the type of disadvantage that would characterize their employment experience, if present, is job mismatch or overqualification. The Labor Utilization Framework has allowed me to investigate this point. In spite of the criticisms that the job mismatch measure has received, it is an objective measure that provides the opportunity to test and measure this notion of Asian disadvantage in the labor market. My research for this book has proven me right on all three points: that Asians are indeed more likely to be underemployed than non-Hispanic whites, that Asians have the highest rates of job mismatch (across race and ethnic groups), and that the odds of underemployment and job mismatch vary across Asian ethnic groups.

This book is organized in a way that imparts the basic arguments and findings of this research efficiently. Chapter 1 lays out the arguments for the research question and discusses the emprical and theoretical background of the research and the conceptual framework. A brief history of Asian immigration to the United States is presented in Chapter 2, to put this research in the context of the larger Asian immigration experience. The data source used in this study, as well as the operationalization of the data and the methods used for analysis, is discussed in Chapter 3. Studying employment outcomes necessarily implies sample selection problems since the people studied are preselected among those who are in the labor force. As such, studying and estimating the probability of labor force participation, as presented in Chapter 4, is a substantive and technical (sample selection correction) procedure. Chapters 5 and 6 provide the results of the research study, dealing with descriptive and multivariate results respectively. Conclusions and recommendations are discussed in Chapter 7.

This book would never have come to fruition without the help and inspiration of a number of people. First, my thanks to Gordon De Jong, Distinguished Professor of Sociology, Pennsylvania State University, who has seen this project through from conceptualization to completion (and beyond!). Amy Preble and Heather Boender of the Carolina Population Center (CPC), University of North Carolina at Chapel Hill, helped in typing earlier drafts of the manuscript and the foreword. Heather's help was invaluable in cross-checking the bibliography with the text. The center's editor Lynn Moody Igoe edited and typeset the manuscript and guided it through its transformation from dissertation to book. CPC reference librarians Mary Jane Hill and Laurie Leadbetter contributed their skills in locating hard-to-find references as did Bernice Bergerup of the university's Walter Royal Davis Library. I thank Tania Bissell, Assistant Editor at Garland Publishing, for her many helpful suggestions for preparing the final camera-ready copy and her successor, Deane Tucker, for his help in the final march toward publication. I would also like to acknowledge the William and Flora Hewlett Foundation, the Andrew Mellon Foundation, the Penn State Population Research Institute, and the Carolina Population Center for the financial and institutional resources made available to me while working on this project. Finally, thanks to my family and friends for the inspiration that pushed me this far and made the completion of this book a reality.

Anna B. Madamba
New York City
February 1998

Underemployment among Asians in the United States

1
Introduction

The labor force integration of minorities in the United States has been at the forefront of economic assimilation research. Minorities are often disadvantaged in gaining access to jobs for which they are educationally qualified (Edwards 1979), earn less than their white counterparts (Chiswick 1986; Tienda and Lii 1987), and are more likely to suffer work discrimination (Edwards 1979). Studies document the economic disadvantage of minority groups, particularly of blacks and Hispanics in terms of underemployment (Lichter 1988) in general, and unemployment (Blau and Ferber 1992; Clogg and Sullivan 1983), working poverty (Gardner and Herz 1992), and job mismatch (Sicherman 1991) in particular.

Asians, like any other minority group in the United States, also are subjected to employment inadequacies. Their plight usually is of less concern since they are seen as economically better off than other minority groups. What is masked in this picture of the economic success of Asians may be issues of employment adequacy, where they may actually have to work longer hours or several jobs to be the economic successes that they are perceived to be. At the same time, this group is not homogenous and can exhibit varied employment experiences by national origin. This study integrates immigration trends and labor market situations into an analysis of the economic assimilation of Asians in the United States. It specifically examines the microlevel determinants of four forms of underemployment (unemployment, part-time work, working poverty, and job mismatch) for white, Indian, Filipino, and Vietnamese men and women in 1980 and 1990.

Background

Contemporary employment issues in the United States address three basic considerations: (1) the changing demographic composition of the workforce, (2) the worker's social well-being, and (3) the shifts in the industrial make-up of the labor market. A study of labor underutilization among Asians in the United States touches on all of these.

First, the impact of changes in the demographic composition of the workforce on employment outcomes is partly attributed to the increase in the number of immigrants to the United States. Between 1965 and 1989, an average of 480 thousand legal immigrants entered the United States each year and of this number, roughly 60 percent were of labor force age (U.S. Naturalization and Immigration Service, various years). During this time period, an increasing proportion of immigrants have come from Asia . In fact, Asians comprise the fastest growing minority group in the United States. The 1980–90 growth rate of the Asian population in the United States was twenty times the rate of non-Hispanic whites, six times that of blacks, and double that of Hispanics (O'Hare and Felt 1991). Projections show that the Asian population of the United States is expected to increase from three million in 1980 to ten million in 2000, an annual increase of 2.4 percent in the proportion of the United States population that is Asian (Bouvier and Agresta 1987). This growth of the Asian population in the United States is anticipated to have an increasing impact on the general employment experience of workers in the United States because of labor competition, differences in human capital accumulation, and the interactive and interdisciplinary nature of work in recent times.

A second facet of the changing employment conditions in the recent past is the growing concern for the social well-being of workers. Current work conditions which include on-site day care, flexible work schedules, paternity and family leaves, and company-assisted spousal employment are all examples of this concern. This growing focus on the general well-being of the worker also is evident in the recent employment literature. In the past, employment research was purely economic, concerned primarily with the determinants of earnings, earnings differentials, unemployment, and the like. Deborah Klein (1973) suggested the need for a social welfare perspective to employment and manpower research, as the result of apprehensions brought about by the increasing poverty experienced not only by the unemployed but by working people as well. These raised concerns regarding the adequacy of employment income for day-to-day survival of certain groups of workers. Since about 90 percent of a household's income is from salaries and wages (Grubb and Wilson 1989), employment outcomes have definite links to the social outcomes of workers and their families. Klein (1973) contends that a more accurate account of the "economic health of the nation" requires the use of other employment indicators that would tap conditions such as racial differences in employment, intermittent employment, and discouraged workers which are usually masked by standard (un)employment or labor force concepts. As minority workers continue to increase and comprise the majority of the labor force, assessing subemployment and labor underuse becomes increasingly important since minority groups are more predisposed to such conditions (Spring 1971).

Third, the participation of the United States in the global economy has brought changes to the industrial composition of the U.S. labor force. The most important impact of the global economy on the U.S. labor market is deindustrialization (Bluestone and Harrison 1982) in which manufacturing jobs are exported to other countries, and the U.S. economy shifts from being goods producing to service producing. This shift of focus has implications for the kind of skills required for jobs in the United States. One such effect is the increased educational qualifications required by jobs, partly through the incorporation of high technology (Noyelle 1987) in even the most simple jobs (e.g., secretarial work). Deindustrialization requires the re-education of the workforce in the United States to keep up to date with the technology boom in the workplace. Another implication of globalization is the exposure of foreign nationals to American culture, trade, and employment partly through mass media and contact with American companies that have exported their businesses and technology overseas. This exposure has significance for the possible migration decisions of foreign nationals, which in turn has an impact on the labor market situation in the United States.

The changing composition of the workforce with the addition of more women, youth, and minorities has implications for underemployment because these groups have historically been disadvantaged in the labor force (Hornbeck and Salamon 1991). Since these groups are more likely to be concentrated in the secondary labor market (Edwards 1979), an increase in their numbers means greater competition and falling wages. At the same time, the decline in manufacturing jobs and the increase in low-skill service jobs translate into unemployment for unskilled workers and low pay for service workers. The emphasis on re-education in response to the onset of high technology in the workplace means that the human capital skills needed to perform well in the labor force are now redefined (Block and Hirschorn 1987; Kanter 1990). This situation has implications for education-job or human capital-employment mismatch (Holzer and Vroman 1992). Today's structural labor market situation in the United States provides a fertile context for the growing importance of studying underemployment.

Significance

While most research on labor force underutilization in the United States has focused on the labor force in general, on whites, or on white-black differences, the increasing racial diversity of the United States offers a new population dynamic for underutilization research. Minority workers have long been identified with marginal work, as reflected in their disadvantaged status in earnings relative to whites (Chiswick 1986), time and work situations (Spring 1971), and access to good jobs (Edwards 1979; Piore 1979). The employment experiences of Asians in the United States provide an interesting innovation to the study of economic assimilation.

Often heralded as the "model minority" (O'Hare and Felt 1991) for their high educational attainment, native-like skills, and hard work, Asians in the United States still seem to be facing impediments that leave them lagging behind the majority white society in economic advancement. Masked by this popular stereotype is the ethnic diversity of the Asian immigrant population (Xenos et al., 1987). Despite the apparent "success" among certain Asian groups, other Asian groups do not have the human capital attributes that contribute to labor market success. Chiswick (1986) found that the mean years of education varied from a high of 17.1 for South Asians to 13.8 for Southeast Asians and that relative to whites, the Japanese had the least earnings differential among Asians, followed by Filipinos, Chinese, and Koreans. In other words, the Asian population in the United States provides a context for employment studies that is different from that of other native and immigrant ethnic minority populations. Lumped together under the label "Asian" are professionals and business entrepreneurs at one extreme, and laborers and service workers at the other. I investigate the range of variability in underemployment across these diverse ethnic groups.

Studying the underemployment experience of specific immigrant groups fills in a research gap by documenting the employment experiences of subpopulations for whom underemployment data were unavailable until the release of the 1980 and 1990 U.S. Census Public-Use Microdata files. Previous research on racial differentials in underemployment has concentrated on black-white differences, and more recently on Hispanic workers in the United States. The availability of data on Asians now allows the investigation of underemployment among a nationally representative sample of Asians in the United States.

Finally, this book documents the intergroup as well as intragroup differentials in the microlevel experience of underemployment by people of different Asian backgrounds. This focus may provide important policy implications by avoiding the fallacy of assuming that all Asian groups in the United States have homogenous economic assimilation experiences. By studying specific Asian groups instead of relying on aggregated Asian group estimates, research results and policy recommendations can be tailored to specific groups.

Theoretical Background and Conceptual Framework

The study of underemployment addresses a new segment in the sociology of work—employment quality and stability (Clogg 1979). Measurement of underemployment dates as far back as 1966 when the Wirtz Subunemployment Index was introduced. By 1978, a total of eight indexes of subemployment or underutilization had been proposed (see Sullivan 1978 for an overview of all eight). While the purposes for the indexes varied, they had three components in common: unemployment, involuntary part-time work, and inadequate income (Sullivan 1978). Philip Hauser formulated the Labor Force Utilization Index (later known as the Labor Utilization Framework or LUF) in the early 1970s.

The first formulation of the LUF covered five components of underutilization: unemployed, underutilized by low income, underutilized by low hours, mismatch, and adequately employed (Hauser 1974). Sullivan (1978) was the first to apply this framework to the U.S. labor force, and introduced innovations to the framework by way of operationalizations for income inadequacy and mismatch. In 1979, Clogg adapted the Sullivan version of the framework, with modifications in the measurement of the income adequacy variable and adding the subunemployed (discouraged workers) as the sixth component to the framework. Clogg and Sullivan (1983) added improvements to the measurement of inadequate income and mismatch by using the 1.25 × poverty threshold figure as the standard cutoff point for measuring income inadequacy and using only individuals who have completed at least twelve years of schooling as a new condition for mismatch.

Further improvements were made to the LUF by Clogg, Sullivan, and Mutchler (1986) based on modifications proposed by Tipps and Gordon (1985). The existing six-component underutilization framework was modified to eleven categories to include subcategories of unemployment and part-time work that reflect specific reasons for these two categories. This reflects an expansion of the original six-category LUF, where there are data to support such; however, the original major LUF categories have remained intact and are the ones used in this study. Results from previous studies reveal that underemployment has increased over the years (Clogg and Sullivan 1983). The economic forms of underemployment (unemployment, involuntary part-time employment, and working with low income) were more prevalent among women and the young. Job mismatch was more likely among men. The gap in underemployment rates of blacks and whites widened in a twelve-year span regardless of age group, education, or temporal macroeconomic shifts (Lichter 1988). In general, a greater likelihood of unemployment is observed for minority groups compared to whites, with blacks and Hispanics also more likely than whites to be working poor (Blau and Ferber 1992; Gardner and Herz 1992). The discussion above shows how underemployment is potentially determined by a number of factors, as it is experienced differently by age, gender, race, and ethnic group; education and skills; and industry and occupation. I analyze these determinants and discuss how they relate to underemployment.

Human Capital

The human capital theory views the acquisition of skills and knowledge as investments of resources on people for future economic payoffs (Becker 1962). Such skills and knowledge are supposed to increase worker productivity, thereby justifying the costs incurred in acquiring them (Salamon 1991). Given this perspective, schooling, on-the-job training, medical care, and anything that affects the productive capacities of the workforce can be considered forms of human capital (Becker 1962; Salamon 1991). Therefore, possession of anything that enhances worker productivity is expected to be translated into socioeconomic rewards. Under the human capital perspective, underemployment is viewed as a result of fewer investments in the type of skills and knowledge mentioned above.

   Whether it is because of its productivity-enhancing effects or its screening/signaling function, additional education is expected to generate a corresponding increase in earnings (Blau and Ferber 1992). However, variations in returns to education by gender (Blau and Ferber 1992; Reskin and Padavic 1994), race (Chiswick 1991; Nelson 1988), and immigrant status (Chiswick 1983) are incongruous findings with human capital theory. Others find that English language capability can discount the effects of education on socioeconomic rewards (Chiswick

1991; Kossoudji 1988; McManus, Gould, and Welch 1983). Under the human capital theory, highly educated Asians are not expected to suffer as much from economic underemployment as they are from mismatch, where the major criterion is high educational background. While whites have the highest returns to human capital characteristics among ethnic groups in the United States, Asians also show favorable returns to human capital characteristics but at rates lower than those of whites (Miller 1992). This can be attributed to the increasing immigration of highly skilled and well-educated Asians in the 1970s (Chiswick 1986) relative to other immigrant groups. In fact, non-Hispanic white, black, and Asian immigrants were more likely than their native-born counterparts to have completed four years of college or more (Meisenheimer 1992). This overachievement in educational attainment has been identified as being responsible for Asian Americans approaching socioeconomic parity with whites (Hirschman and Wong 1984). The Japanese, Indians, and Chinese are among the most economically settled of the Asian groups in the United States (Chiswick 1983; Nelson 1988). The Vietnamese are the least advantaged by virtue of their lower human capital investments rather than the recency of their migration (Nelson 1988).

Demographic processes and changing labor markets are expected to alter the influence of human capital investments on labor market status. Technological advancement, expanded international competition, changing economic structure, and increased pressure for productivity improvements are demand-side factors that can affect the influence of human capital investment on labor market status. On the other hand, the baby boomers' overload of retirement systems, the corresponding birth dearth leading to an overburdened dependency ratio, and the changing workforce composition of mostly minorities, women, and immigrants are demographic challenges affecting the supply side of human capital investment (Reskin and Padavic 1994; Salamon 1991). Given the above, the observed growth in the number of college graduates plus the economy's inability to absorb them has reduced the returns to education in general, and increased the potential for a mismatch between the labor demanded by industry and the labor supplied by educational institutions (Salamon 1991).

Family and Household Structure

Changing trends in marriage, fertility, life expectancy, and labor force participation have altered the labor market situation for today's workers.

Increasing divorce rates, the rise in female-headed households, increased female labor force participation, as well as delayed childbearing have all contributed to a workplace situation where workers, especially women, are faced with conditions necessitating employment (as in single-parent households), but hampered by these same conditions from pursuing employment (as in care for young children). As a result, they face a conflict between work and family re-sponsibilities that is often addressed through modified work practices (shift work, flexible time, part-time work, and other solutions) or at the expense of family life. This conflict between work and family responsibilities is critical in the study of underemployment. Family and household situations can influence not only labor force participation but also the availability and desirability of jobs.

Child care may be the most important component in this work-family quandry. Increased opportunities for women brought about by the growth in the service sector (Presser 1989), as well as men's declining labor market position (Wilkie 1991), have made participation in the labor force an attractive option for women—born either out of choice and ambition, or need and survival. In fact, female labor force participation grew over 30 percent between 1940 and 1990, including half of married women with young children (Blau and Ferber 1992). This figure implies that demand for child care is expected to be huge as more mothers join the workforce. The availability of institutional and noninstitutional child care will determine whether women join the labor force. In spite of the general trend of increasing labor force participation among women, the presence of young children (Blau and Ferber 1992) and the inavailability of satisfactory child care (Blau and Robins 1989) remain a deterrent for a number of women from joining the workforce. Other women compromise by working only part-time (Blau and Ferber 1992), part-year (Hayghe and Bianchi 1994), or working at night and on shifts (Presser 1986). The child care woes of married women look insignificant when compared to the problems faced by female-headed households. Single household-heads are confronted by the double responsibility of earning a living and caring for a child. Given the dampening effect of children on labor force participation, women have fewer options for jobs resulting in lower income and high incidences of poverty among this type of household (Blau and Ferber 1992). The underemployment rate for single mothers is 53 percent, twice that of other women and four times that of men (Sheets, Nord, and Phelps 1987).

It has been established in the literature that the shift in women's labor force participation is because of the rise in the wage rate and the decrease in the value of time at home. These conditions contributed to increasing the opportunity cost of staying at home compared to being in the labor force. However, the declining economic status of men also contributes to the increase in women's labor force participation (Wilkie 1991). In fact, the proportion of families wherein the man is the sole breadwinner declined 27 percent between 1960 and 1988 (Wilkie 1991). One in five married white men and one in three married black men have earnings insufficient to support a family of four above the poverty line (Wilkie 1991). The number of men with income close to the median wage has shrunk through the disappearance of jobs near the middle of the male distribution. In short, men are losing middle-class jobs while women are not (Burtless 1990). Therefore, the role of additional earners in the family has grown in importance for the economic vitality of the household.

Having more than one worker in a family dramatically lowers the probability of poverty (Klein and Rones 1989). The wife is usually the second breadwinner in the family, and her income sometimes determines whether a family or household will live above or below the poverty threshold. Having an employed wife usually increases family income by an average of 42 percent among whites and 67 percent among blacks (Blau and Ferber 1992). Poverty reduction through secondary earners is greater among immigrant than native families (Jensen 1991). Whites, blacks, and Hispanic immigrant families are better off because of the ameliorative impact of secondary earners (Jensen 1991). The role of secondary earners in Asian families and households is significant since 18 percent of Asian families have three or more workers compared to 14 percent for non-Hispanic white families (O'Hare and Felt 1991). The ameliorative effect of secondary earners is seen for native and immigrant Asian families (Jensen 1991).

This discussion shows that a combination of family and household factors can undermine labor market activity. Having a child can work to reduce labor activity, particularly for women, forcing them to leave the labor force, be unemployed, or work part-time. Having supplemental earners can help families rise above the poverty threshold.

Industrial Sector

Structural changes in the labor market brought about by American deindustrialization has implications for underemployment. Economic restructuring featuring a shift from a goods-producing to a service-producing economy has changed the supply and demand for jobs. At the same time, the previously mentioned demographic changes have altered the composition of workers in these jobs.

Economic restructuring is best characterized by the disinvestment in the basic productive industries in the country (Bluestone and Harrison 1982). This is evidenced by the growth of high-technology industries and the increasing role of information technology in all aspects of industry (Etzioni and Jargowsky 1990; Noyelle 1987), coupled with the increasing flight of capital and the relocation of manufacturing industries overseas (Bluestone and Harrison 1982).

These trends can be attributed to two major developments in the recent past—the increased competitiveness of the global economy and the advances in technological development, particularly in information technology (Bluestone and Harrison 1982; Noyelle 1987). The 1970s saw the advent of increased competition from abroad in virtually every U.S. major industry (Bluestone and Harrison 1982). As a consequence, U.S. firms had to face the reality of shrinking profits unless they reacted with cost-cutting/price-reducing measures. This profit-squeeze situation was aggravated by the postwar string of union victories that continued until the 1970s (Bluestone and Harrison 1982), and the recessions that plagued the United States in the 1980s (Freedman 1985). In the light of reduced industry profits, management responded by relocating some operations overseas, where labor is cheap. Advances in technology contributed to making this a feasible decision by facilitating the remittance of money, use of telecommunications, and improved and efficient transportation systems.

On top of its contribution to the capital mobility that led to the movement of manufacturing industries out of the United States, technological development had an impact on economic restructuring in another way by causing the reorganization of work in the workplace. The changes included the development of skill requirements from processing skills to problem-solving skills, increased importance attached to education at all levels, the development of an interdisciplinary nature of work, increased desire for more creative contributions to the work, and manpower training from external sources (Noyelle 1987).

One implication of this transformation is a rise in service-sector jobs (Burtless 1990). High concentrations of sales, clerical, and service occupations are found in the service industry compared to manufacturing, and they have traditionally been low-wage, unsheltered occupations with low levels of professionalization, unionization, and institutional credentialling. Although there is no evidence of the impact of the service industry as a whole on structural underemployment, retail and social service sectors increase part-time underemployment while advanced corporate services and retail services also increased low wage underemployment (Sheets et al. 1987). At the same time, the flight of manufacturing jobs meant the disappearance of many middle management positions, particularly for men (Burtless 1990). A result is the displacement of unskilled workers who do not have the training to perform even low-skilled jobs, and the underemployment of other workers with increased educational backgrounds and skills. Most profoundly hit by deindustrialization are black men, who faced rising unemployment in the 1970s following the decline in manufacturing (Holzer and Vroman 1992). A consequence of these changes in the occupational structure is a split society (Bellin and Miller 1990) characterized by the polarization of jobs into low-skilled service jobs and high-skilled, high-technology ones.

The focus on higher education and high-technology skills means that people without them will be dislocated from jobs. This situation has a negative impact on Asian immigrants who lack such skills and on new immigrants who would otherwise have outdated skills. In general, the impact of the transformation of the workplace for Asians should be the same for whites and blacks as well, given the same qualifications. It does not specifically favor Asians, but given the focus on education, the impact is stronger among Asians and whites (and less for blacks), mainly because of the proportion of the population that is highly educated and in the labor force.

The industries and occupations that Asians in the United States are involved in generally follow those of non-Hispanic whites. They are more likely to work in manufacturing and trade and less likely to be found in farming, fishing, mining, and construction (O'Hare and Felt 1991). Asians are more likely than non-Hispanic whites to have managerial and professional positions,and less likely to be in blue-collar occupations (O'Hare and Felt 1991). Their high educational attainment has therefore found them a place in the postindustrial United States, with the skills demanded in high-technology jobs. However, other labor market forces operate to affect the total economic assimilation of Asians in the labor market. There is evidence of peripherization of Asian immigrant professionals to areas where native-born workers would prefer not to work (Shin and Chang 1988).

Assimilation

One demographic change affecting the labor market is the rise in the number of immigrants seeking jobs. In fact, immigrants (together with women and minorities) are expected to comprise a greater portion of the new pool of workers in the United States (Salamon 1991). Immigrants are known to experience disadvantage in the labor market immediately following their move because of the absence of location-specific capital (DaVanzo 1981). However, they are expected to reach employment parity with native-born workers the longer they stay in the country. Economic assimilation is achieved when immigrants have the same economic opportunities as native-born workers, and the returns to human capital investments in terms of earnings and occupational status are the same for both groups.

There is a substantial gap in earnings and occupational status between natives and immigrants, one that is reduced as one ages (Meisenheimer 1992). Deficits in returns to education, age, and experiences account for a large fraction of this gap (Ko and Clogg 1989). However, earnings returns to human capital attributes do improve with time. Tang (1993) finds that among engineers, Asian engineers take six to eleven years to catch up with Caucasians in earnings while the first ten years of experience in the United States was found to raise earnings of immigrants by more than 20 percent (Lalonde and Topel 1990). Positive gains of length of residence on occupational status were found to have occurred within five to ten years for Japanese, twenty years for Indians, and thirty years for Koreans and Filipinos (Nelson 1988). This evidence shows that the labor market position of immigrants gets better with time, but there is no direct evidence that immigrants reach economic parity with whites. Although Asian women were found to have earnings equal to whites, this was attributed to their overachievement in education (Wong and Hirschman 1983). In all age groups and at all educational levels, non-Hispanic white men earned more money than Asian men with the same age and educational characteristics, a trend followed by non-Hispanic white and Asian women as well (O'Hare and Felt 1991).

One detrimental factor inhibiting full economic assimilation of immigrants is English language proficiency. McManus and colleagues (1983) find that English language deficiency can reduce the income that is ordinarily associated with schooling and work experience. This deficiency not only affects earnings, but has negative repercussions for occupational opportunities as well (Koussoudji 1988). These abilities are expected to improve, with increased duration in the United States. The detrimental effect of language difficulties is stronger for Hispanics than Asians, with Asians at all skill levels losing very little when they are deficient in English (Koussoudji 1988).

Earnings equality, access to similar jobs in the core sector, and comparable chances for occupational mobility between natives and immigrants all point to full economic assimilation in the labor force. In spite of Asian immigrants being incorporated into the American labor force in jobs and industries that can be considered attractive, full economic assimilation is still lacking. For the most part, full economic assimilation is observed for native-born offspring of immigrants, particularly the Chinese and Japanese (Chiswick 1983).

In summary, this review shows that a number of factors affect people's labor force chances, leading to underemployment. Underemployment outcomes are theoretically linked to the four groups of independent variables discussed earlier as well as some demographic controls. Human capital, family and household, industry sector, demographic, and migration and language indicators of assimilation are hypothesized to affect the different underemployment outcomes based on the conceptual framework presented in Figure 1.1. The influence of the human capital, family and household, industry, migration and language, and demographic variables on underemployment outcomes are direct and mediated through the selective process of labor force participation decision making. Education plays an important role in landing a job as do skills and English language capacity. Education is expected to decrease the likelihood of the economic forms of underemployment, but increase the chances of job mismatch, particularly for the immigrant groups. Disability impairs or reduces labor activity, increasing the likelihood for unemployment or part-time employment. Family and household structures can work towards inhibiting labor force participation as well as facilitating underemployment, particularly for women. Part-time employment, job mismatch, or working poverty are expected to increase to accommodate family compromises. Industrial restructuring determines the occupational make-up of the labor market, subsequently determining the structure of jobs and wages. Industries characterized by low-skilled jobs, low wages, and high turnover rates, are expected to incorporate a great many economically underemployed workers. Finally, immigrant status can be detrimental to socioeconomic advancement, at least in the short term, which could lead to increased chances of all forms of underemployment.

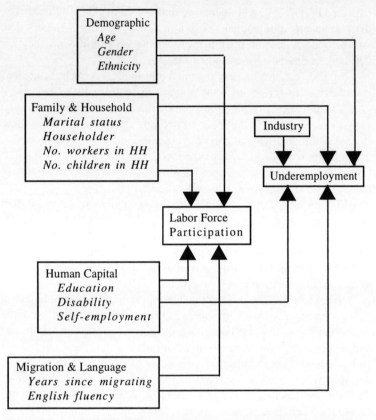

Figure 1.1   Conceptual framework for the microlevel study of Asian underemployment

Objectives

This book focuses on underemployment as a form of economic well-being among the Asian minority group. That the labor force participation of Asians is increasing rapidly makes a study of under-employment very suitable to this particular ethnic group. In fact, O'Hare and Felt (1991:15) state that "while Asian Americans are often viewed as an economic success story, evidence suggests that they are still not rewarded at a level one would expect given their educational attainment." By looking specifically at three Asian groups (Indians, Filipinos, and the Vietnamese, with whites as a reference group) with different human capital and employment profiles, I address the following questions: (1) How prevalent is underemployment among Asians in the United States? How different are the underemployment experiences of specific Asian groups from each other and from those of whites? (2) What are the determinants of the different forms of underemployment for each group and how do these determinants vary across groups? (3) To what extent does recent migration and English language proficiency affect the experience of underemployment? (4) Are there differential returns to human capital across Asian groups as was found in previous research? Are there gender differences in the influences of human capital on underemployment within and between groups? (5) How do family considerations affect the underemployment experiences of the Asian groups in this book? Is the influence of family and household variables the same between gender and within and among Asian groups? and, (6) Is there any difference in the underemployment experience of Asians in the United States between 1980 and 1990? I hope to address these questions and shed light into the underemployment experience of specific Asian groups in the United States.

2

Asian Immigration
to the United States

Immigrants come to the United States for various reasons. While economic reasons rank high among the motivating factors, they are not the sole reason. The reason for immigrating and the mode of entry into the United States can determine the type of labor activity (Portes 1981) and the way it is pursued. People on working visas are recruited for their qualifications and skill and are therefore quite adequately placed in the labor market. Permanent residents admitted by virtue of family reunification or refugee status must compete with residents in the domestic labor market. Temporary visitors like tourists cannot legally work in the United States and may have to settle for subemployment or peripheral economy employment because of the legal restrictions on their employment. Students and exchange scholars can work under specific guidelines, in areas limited to their educational venture. Given the variety of possible reasons for coming to the United States, it is essential to analyze the immigration background of Asian labor force streams to explain better their labor market outcomes in the United States. Entry status can reflect, in part, what human capital characteristics migrants possess, their family situation, and their resources for job searches. These characteristics help determine the labor market incorporation expected from the groups studied.

Immigration to the United States:
A Brief History

The United States has always been known as an immigrant nation. The volume of people immigrating to this nation since the early 1800s is shown in Figure 2.1. Northwestern Europeans dominated the immigrant stream to the United States during most of the nineteenth century (U.S. Immigration and Naturalization Service 1991a). Economic, social, and political problems in Europe spurred this first wave of migration, predominantly originating from Germany, Ireland, and the United Kingdom.

Millions

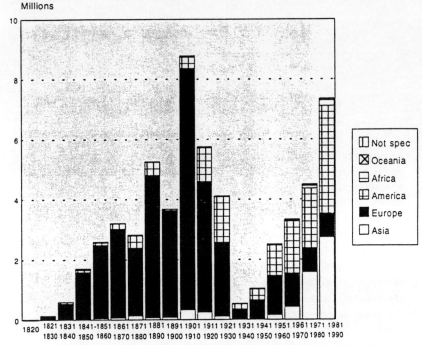

Figure 2.1 Immigration to the United States by region and year

The year 1880 marked a rapid increase in the number of immigrants admitted to the United States. This increase was accounted for not by more Northwestern Europeans but by "new immigrants" who came increasingly from Southeastern Europe, particularly Italy, Russia, and Austria-Hungary (U.S. Naturalization and Immigration Service 1991). The late 1800s also marked the first wave of Asian immigrants coming to the United States, particularly from South China (Arnold, Minocha, and Fawcett 1987). These new immigrants provided the manpower needed to compensate for a labor shortage plaguing the United States at that time.

World War I led to a decline in immigration, but it was followed by an increase after the war, usually of European war refugees. By the time this immigration peaked in the 1920s, the United States was experiencing economic difficulties, part of which were repercussions of the war. People demanded a limit to immigration. The Quota Act of

1921 answered these demands by providing national numerical limits to immigration. This quota law (and subsequent amendments/addenda) favored Northern and Western European immigrants and was unfavorable to Asians, Africans, Australians, and Southeastern Europeans. Immigration in the 1930s fell to a record low during the Great Depression. The absence of economic opportunities in the United States not only reduced immigration to its lowest point since the early 1800s, but also marked an increase in emigration rates (U.S. Immigration and Naturalization Service 1991a). While immigration and naturalization continued under the Quota Act, the onset of World War II again reduced immigration to the United States. However, wartime labor shortages in the United States called for importing temporary workers from neighboring countries, particularly Mexico (U.S. Immigration and Naturalization Service 1991a). This situation sparked a migrant labor agreement between the United States and Mexico that later developed into the Bracero Program. This program, coupled with war refugees, communist escapees, illegal immigrants, and more recent refugees comprised the source of the rising immigration trend immediately after World War II.

The 1965 Amendment to the Immigration and Naturalization Act abolished the national origins system and set country numerical quotas based on family reunification preferences and immigrant skills to match labor force demands in the United States (U.S. Immigration and Naturalization Service 1991a). This act precipitated a marked escalation in immigration and opened the doors of the United States to groups that had previously been restricted. The current wave of Asian immigration started with the 1965 change in the Immigration and Naturalization Act.

Legislation and Asian Immigration to the United States

Asians are currently the fastest growing minority group in the United States (Arnold et al. 1987; O'Hare and Felt 1991). The long history of Asian immigration to the United States can be traced as far back as the 1800s (Figure 2.2). During the first wave of immigration to the United States, when Europeans comprised the bulk of the immigrants, the first Asian immigrants also started coming (U.S. Immigration and Naturalization Service 1989). Chinese, Japanese, and Indians made up the Asian population in the United States during the mid- to late 1880s. Relatively large numbers of Chinese began immigrating in the early to mid-1880s to cover labor shortages and work on the railroads (Arnold et al. 1987).

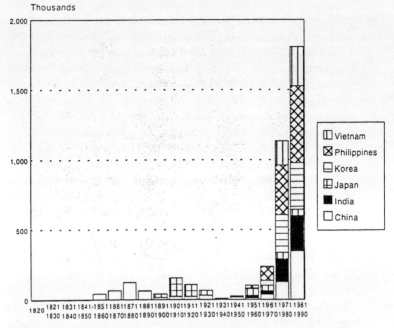

Figure 2.2   Immigrants to the United States from six major Asian countries: 1820–1990

However, their tendency to keep to themselves and not to assimilate, bred anti-Chinese sentiments, resulting in the Chinese Exclusion Act of 1892 (Bouvier and Gardner 1986) which barred additional Chinese laborers from immigrating to the United States.

The Japanese dominated Asian immigration from the late 1880s to 1917 and were also recruited for labor on the farms of Hawaii and California. However, like the Chinese before them, problems of assimilation resulted to a similar exclusionary move, known as the 1907 Gentleman's Agreement with Japan. In response to the crisis brought about by rising immigration in the face of economic troubles, the Immigration Act of 1917 was passed. One of its provisions was the exclusion of persons from the "Asiatic Barred Zone," which covered most of Asia and the Pacific Islands (U.S. Immigration and Naturalization Service 1991a). The Quota Act of 1921 installed national origin numerical limits to immigrants from different countries, an approach unfavorable for Asian immigrants (U.S. Immigration and Naturalization Service 1991a). Although Asian immigration has been restricted by United States legislation, a few concessions have also been provided. In 1943, the Chinese Exclusion Act was repealed, and eligibility for citizenship was extended to natives of India and the Philippines in 1946 (U.S. Immigration and Naturalization Service 1991a). Similarly, the McCarran-Walter Act of 1952 revised immigration regulations for Asians and set up quotas for the Asian-Pacific triangle (Arnold et al. 1987). Asian immigration, however, remained low relative to the other groups in the United States. It did not escalate until the 1965 Amendment to the Immigration and Naturalization Act (Figure 2.2).

Divergent Pathways to the United States: Indians, Filipinos, and Vietnamese

The passing of the 1965 Amendment to the Immigration and Naturalization Act together with the repercussions of the Vietnam War shaped the post-1965 Asian immigration picture (Arnold et al. 1987). As for most of the other Asian groups, Indian, Filipino, and Vietnamese immigration increased drastically after the passing of the 1965 legislation (Figure 2.3). At the same time, the rise in Vietnamese immigrants also was brought about by repercussions of the war. Table 2.1 shows the average annual growth rates of immigrants admitted to the United States from India, the Philippines, and Vietnam. They range from a high of 26 percent per year between 1960 and 1970, to a low of 4 percent per year between 1980 and 1990. Of note is the high 37 percent annual growth rate of Vietnamese immigrants between 1970 and 1980, reflecting the refugee stream resulting from the Vietnam War. Although their absolute numbers are still well below those of other minority groups in the United States, Asians are now the fastest growing minority group with rates twenty times that of non-Hispanic whites, six times that of blacks, and twice that of Hispanics (O'Hare and Felt 1991). They are projected to number as many as twenty million in 2030 (Bouvier and Agresta 1987). What are the origins of this population? A look at the immigration experiences of Indians, Filipinos, and Vietnamese follows.

Indians in the United States: Brain Drain?

Indian immigrants to the United States in the early 1900s were students (Melendy 1977) and construction and farm workers (Minocha 1987). Their numbers did not increase much because of discrimination experiences which led to exclusion legislation in 1917 (Melendy 1977; Minocha 1987). Indian immigration did not increase again until 1946, when Indians were given citizenship (Minocha 1987). Immigrants after

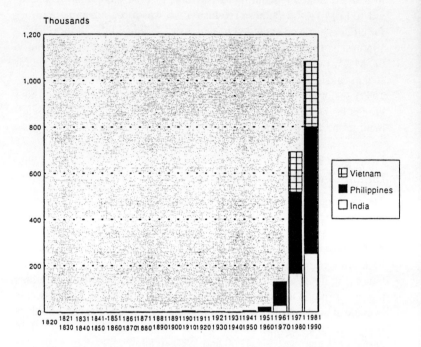

Thousands

Figure 2.3   Immigrants to the United States from India, the Philipppines, and Vietnam: 1820–1990

World War II were mostly professionals and their families (Melendy 1977). The inception of economic and political relations between India and the United States in the 1940s promoted technical assistance through training skilled Indian personnel in new technology. This flight of educated and highly skilled Indians for training started the highly educated Indian population base in the United States, as most of those immigrants decided not to go home (Minocha 1987). The 1965 changes in immigration legislation allowed the continued influx of Indians, initially under occupational preferences but increasingly under relative or family preferences. This background on Indian immigration establishes the predominantly highly educated and professional base that characterizes the Indian population in the United States. Studies that Minocha (1987) cites show that most Indians are professionals with high labor force participation rates, high levels of education, and high incomes. However, there is evidence of underemployment, especially

Table 2.1 Increase in the population of immigrants admitted to the United States from selected Asian countries between 1951 and 1990

	Increase					
	1951–60 to 1961–70		*1961–70 to 1971–80*		*1971–80 to 1981–90*	
Country	*No.*	*r[a]*	*No.*	*r[a]*	*No.*	*r[a]*
All	806198	2.78	1171637	3.02	2844748	4.91
India	25216	26.23	136945	17.98	86652	4.24
Philippines	79069	16.28	256611	12.80	193777	4.36
Vietnam	4005	25.62	168480	36.84	107962	4.85

Source: *Statistical Yearbook of the Immigration and Naturalization Service, 1990*

[a]The average growth rate per annum is computed as: $r = [\log (P_n/P_0)]/ n \log e$, where $e = 2.71828$.

among the professional occupations. Indians were either not employed in their specialty occupations, or if they were, they usually occupied the less prestigious positions (Minocha 1987).

Filipinos in the United States: A Colonial Past

Ties of the Philippines to the United States started in 1898 when the islands were ceded by Spain to the United States under the Treaty of Paris (Pido 1986). From that time until 1934, Filipinos were able to move in, out, and around the United States freely as nationals (Cariño 1987). During the early 1900s, Filipinos were recruited as agricultural laborers for farms in the West and in Hawaii. Most of these early immigrants had little formal education and limited language capabilities (Melendy 1977). However, a small number of more educated Filipinos were sent to the United States as students under an educational program. Immigration virtually stopped after 1934, when Filipinos became subject to the exclusionary laws that had affected the Chinese, Japanese, and Indians earlier. Subsequent Filipino immigrants comprised those naturalized under the 1946 provisions (similar to the Indians) and their dependents.

The 1965 amendment to the immigration laws fostered increased immigration among Filipinos. Unlike the earlier waves of Filipino immigration, however, this post-1965 wave consisted of highly educated and skilled individuals employed in professional occupations (Cariño 1987). Exposure to the American educational system seemed to have facilitated integration into the labor force as well as promoting the passage of students to the United States for advanced training. The continued presence of military bases in the country (up to 1991) also may have influenced immigration to the United States through intermarriages between American servicemen and Filipino nationals and the recruitment of Filipino servicemen for the U.S. military (Cariño 1987). Therefore, the post-1965 Filipino population in the United States is a result of family ties to the initial Filipino settlers who became citizens; professionals who immigrated; those who came on student visas who later adjusted their visa status to working, permanent resident, or something else; and dependents of military servicemen. It also is a result of the continuing recruitment of skilled workers and workers in demand in the United States.

The typical Filipino immigrant to the United States in 1980 is highly educated with an excellent record of civilian labor force participation, and is employed in the technical, sales, or service sectors. The Filipino immigrant was competitive in the labor market, but usually at lower-level jobs, for which they are often overqualified (Pido 1986).

The Vietnamese in the United States: The Refugee Experience

Vietnamese immigration, which was documented starting in 1951 (U.S. Immigration and Naturalization Service 1988) and was not significant until the early 1970s (Gordon 1987). The fall of South Vietnam on April 30, 1975, distinguishes the two general migration waves from Vietnam to the United States. Pre-1975 Vietnamese immigration was composed large-ly of students sent to the United States under U.S. government sponsorship, or spouses of American servicemen stationed in Vietnam (Gordon 1987). Post-1975 immigration is the refugee wave, divided into two parts. The first wave consisted of refugees evacuated immed-iately following the fall of Saigon, when the United States resettled about 130 thousand Vietnamese refugees in resettlement camps (Gordon 1987). This first wave of refugees was better educated, wealthier, spoke English, and had political connections to the United States and many were easy to accommodate because they had relatives in the United States (Rutledge 1992). The succeeding waves of refugees had fled Vietnam and were sent to refugee-processing centers in neighboring countries before resettlement in the United States. This group was ethnically more diverse, poorer, had English language dif-ficulties, and no kin network in the United States (Rutledge 1992). The second wave of immigrants posed a challenge for assimilation. Vietnamese refugees were found to have low overall labor force participation rates, high unemployment rates, low wages, and high use of cash assistance (Gordon 1987). Data show however, that these rates tend to improve through time. The first-wave refugees had positive labor market experiences while the later wave had a more difficult time becoming integrated into the labor force (Gordon 1987). Vietnamese refugees in general have experienced downward occupational mobility, with the nonprofessionals employed disproportionately in low-skilled jobs (Gordon 1987).

Recent Trends in Indian, Filipino, and Vietnamese Immigration

The Refugee Act of 1980, the Immigration Reform and Control Act of 1986, and the Immigration Act of 1990 were enacted to process refugees more efficiently, curb illegal immigration, and revamp preference categories, respectively (U.S. Immigration and Naturalization Service 1991a). The Refugee Act of 1980 provided guidelines for admitting refugees of "special humanitarian concern" to the United States and for providing effective resettlement for those admitted (United States House of Representatives 1980). The Immigration Reform and Control Act of 1986 was designed to control illegal immigration through employer sanctions and increased enforcement (United States House of Representatives 1986). It also has provisions for granting temporary resident status to seasonal agricultural workers and amnesty to those who entered the U.S. illegally before January 1, 1982 (Bouvier and Gardner 1986). The highlight of the U.S. Immigration Act of 1990 was to encourage the immigration of highly skilled workers by the creation of a new category called "priority workers," for which 40 thousand green cards were allocated. These include persons of extraordinary ability, outstanding professors and researchers, and multinational executives and managers, and their accompanying relatives (Siegel and Canter 1990). A second new category, with an allotment of another 40 thousand green cards for "professionals with advanced degrees or persons of exceptional ability," also is a provision of the 1990 act as a means to recruit highly skilled workers (Siegel and Canter 1990). At the same time, the allotment of green cards to unskilled workers was cut by half (Siegel and Canter 1990). An additional feature is the special naturalization benefits for Filipino war veterans as accorded in the Immigration Act of 1990. These provisions combine to determine the recent (as well as future) trends of Asian immigration to the United States.

A review of the basic demographic characteristics of immigrants helps point to their potential incorporation in the labor force through their labor force participation rates, employment sectors, and occupations. Table 2.2 shows these basic demographic characteristics of immigrants from India, the Philippines, and Vietnam. The gender distribution of Asian Indians is more or less equal between 1979 and 1990, with men having a slight edge. On the other hand, there were more women than men immigrants admitted from the Philippines throughout the same time frame. The Vietnamese began by having more men than women immigrants, although the trend has changed since 1990. While immi-

Table 2.2   Sex and age distribution of immigrants to the United States from selected Asian countries: 1979, 1985, 1990

	Sex distribution (%)		Under age 30 (%)	
Country	Male	Female	Male	Female
All countries				
1979	47.6	52.3	62.5	60.5
1985	50.2	49.8	61.5	59.3
1990	53.3	46.7	49.8	49.4
India				
1979	50.7	49.3	59.6	68.5
1985	51.2	48.8	55.7	56.8
1990	50.2	49.7	44.8	50.1
Philippines				
1979	39.5	60.5	51.3	64.6
1985	41.1	58.9	55.1	51.3
1990	40.5	59.5	46.2	42.9
Vietnam				
1979	53.9	46.1	72.9	69.6
1985	57.7	42.3	73.4	64.9
1990	48.0	51.9	68.7	55.5

Source: *Statistical Yearbook of the U.S. Immigration and Naturalization Service,* 1979 (Table 9); 1985 (Table IMM4.3); and 1990 (Tables 12, 14).

Note: No gender and age data available for 1980.

grants are generally known to be young, Table 2.2 shows that the percentage of immigrants below age 30 progressively decreased between 1979 and 1990 for all groups. Indian and Filipino men had lower percentages in the young ages, while the Vietnamese in general were young, with an average of 60 percent of the immigrants admitted under age 30 in 1990.

Unlike the years immediately preceding the 1965 amendment, at least three-quarters of the immigrants were admitted under the family reunification category instead of the occupational preference categories (Table 2.3). The proportion admitted through the family preference category increased for Indians and Vietnamese but decreased for Filipinos between 1979 and 1990. Those admitted through the family preference class were predominantly under the second (unmarried sons and daughters of resident aliens and their children) and fifth (brothers and sisters of U.S. citizens, their spouses and children) preference categories. Interestingly, Indians had a higher proportion of immigrants admitted through the high-skilled occupational preference category compared to Filipinos and Vietnamese. However, this proportion decreased between 1979 and 1990 for Indians and increased for Filipinos and Vietnamese. Higher percentages of sixth preference "workers in short supply" were admitted from the Philippines and Vietnam between 1979 and 1990, than from India. These results show that most of the immigrants admitted to the United States from India, the Philippines, and Vietnam were admitted under the relative preference category, with no special requirements for skill or worker qualifications. Among those admitted for employment in the United States, Indians were mostly admitted in the highly skilled classification, with Filipinos and Vietnamese mostly among workers in short supply.

Table 2.4 shows the distribution of immigrants admitted by occupational group. While more than 50 percent of the immigrants admitted were housewives, children, or the unemployed, employed Indian and Filipino workers were predominantly in professional and technical occupations, while Vietnamese were predominantly in operative, laborer, and transport occupations. Declines in professional and technical employment are evident between 1979 and 1990 for Indians and Vietnamese, but not for Filipinos. In the 1990s Indians find themselves increasingly in managerial and administrative and in service occupations, Filipinos are employed in service and clerical/administrative support occupations, and Vietnamese in operatives, service, and precision production occupations. A job hierarchy is evident—Indians are employed in high-skilled occupations such as professional, technical,

Table 2.3 Immigrants admitted under numerical limitations, by country of origin and class of admission, 1980, 1985, and 1990

Preference category	India			Philippines			Vietnam		
	1980	1985	1990	1980	1985	1990	1980	1985	1990
Total immigrants	19,628	18,833	19,157	19,554	19,490	19,588	4,282	3,755	8,829
Relative preference: Total[a]	83.2	82.5	84.4	98.3	81.1	79.6	37.5	98.0	97.7
1st preference[b]	1.1	0.1	0.3	5.1	22.7	27.1	0.9	2.9	9.8
2nd preference[b]	23.6	48.0	39.6	92.8	36.6	31.8	55.2	58.7	33.6
4th preference[b]	6.6	2.1	5.4	0.4	12.3	12.8	2.2	5.8	12.4
5th preference[b]	75.6	49.8	54.7	1.7	28.4	28.4	41.7	32.6	44.1
Occupational preference: Total[a]	16.7	17.5	15.5	1.6	18.8	20.3	1.8	2.0	0.6
3rd preference[b]	46.1	54.5	34.2	21.9	11.0	13.1	11.5	13.5	37.0
3rd(a) preference[b]	42.9	1.7	34.4	42.1	36.7	35.0	28.2	17.6	18.5
6th preference[b]	6.8	1.1	13.3	21.9	24.6	27.6	20.5	24.3	22.2
6th(a) preference[b]	4.2	1.3	18.2	14.1	27.7	24.3	1.3	44.6	22.2
Other: Total[a,c]	0.04	0.00	0.05	0.09	0.03	0.07	60.7	0.00	1.6

Source: *Statistical Yearbook of the Immigration and Naturalization Service*, 1980, 1985, 1990 (Table 5 for 1980, 1990; Table IMM 2.1 for 1985).

[a]Percentages based on total immigrant population from each country.

[b]Percentages based on total for each general preference category (relative or occupational).

[c]"Other" category includes suspension of deportation adjustments, nonpreference adjustments, private law adjustments, and foreign government official adjustments that are subject to numerical limitations; for 1980, the "other" category also included 7th preference immigrants who are comprised of conditional entrants adjusted and refugees adjusted.

Note: 1st preference—unmarried sons and daughters of U.S. citizens and their children; 2nd preference—spouses, unmarried sons and daughters of resident aliens and their children; 3rd preference—immigrants in professional or highly skilled professions; 3rd(a) preference—dependents of 3rd preference immigrants; 4th preference—married sons and daughters of U.S. citizens, their spouses and children; 5th preference—brothers and sisters of U.S. citizens, their spouses and children; 6th preference—6th(a) preference—dependents of 6th preference immigrants.

Table 2.4 Percentage of immigrants admitted by country of birth and major occupational group: 1979, 1985, and 1990

Occupational group	India			Philippines			Vietnam		
	1979[a]	1985	1990	1979[a]	1985	1990	1979[a]	1985	1990
Total immigrants	19708	26026	30667	41300	47978	63756	22546	31895	48792
Professional & technical	18.7	15.4	12.4	12.0	11.5	14.9	5.6	1.6	1.6
Managerial & administrative	4.8	5.1	6.4	3.9	4.8	5.5	1.7	0.4	0.4
Sales	0.9	1.7	1.4	0.8	2.0	1.7	0.7	1.1	3.7
Clerical/administrative support	3.1	2.1	3.6	3.8	4.0	6.6	4.8	0.9	0.6
Precision production/crafts	1.4	1.6	1.2	2.1	3.0	2.6	4.6	4.5	8.0
Operatives, laborers & transport	1.7	0.9	1.1	3.9	2.5	2.8	14.0	10.9	8.6
Farm	2.6	3.1	4.1	11.2	3.0	2.7	0.4	1.0	4.4
Service	1.0	2.8	4.5	7.6	7.2	7.7	4.2	4.7	6.1
Housewife, children, no occupation	65.7	67.0	65.2	61.4	62.0	55.4	64.1	74.9	66.6

Source: *Statistical Yearbook of the Immigration and Naturalization Service*, 1979, 1985, and 1990 (Tables 8, IMM6.1, and 20, respectively).

[a]Figures for 1980 not available.

managerial, and administrative positions, Filipinos have mid-level employment in professional and technical, service, and clerical/administrative support, and Vietnamese are in low-level jobs in operatives, precision production, and service.

Asian Immigration to the United States: A Summary

This chapter has documented the history of immigration to the United States, showing how different backgrounds, experiences, and legislation shape the immigrant population in the United States, and documenting Indian, Filipino, and Vietnamese immigration trends. An immigration stream comprised of occupational- and educational-category individuals characterizes the experience of Indians in the United States. Filipinos exposed to an American educational system and the presence of American military bases as well as highly skilled individuals characterizes the migration stream from the Philippines. Finally, the Vietnamese population in the United States is mostly a result of the refugee flow following the Vietnam War.

Recent immigration trends give an indication of the future composition of immigrants from these Asian groups. Indians of both genders are equally likely to be immigrants to the United States, with about half of them below age 30. While most Indians are admitted under the relative preference categories, compared to Filipinos and Vietnamese, they have a higher percentage admitted for their exceptional skills. This is reflected in their predominantly professional, technical, managerial, and administrative occupations. Filipinos, on the other hand are mostly women, and older, and are found in professional and technical as well as in service occupations. The Vietnamese show an increasing proportion of women immigrants as well as the very young. They find themselves incorporated in operative, laborer, and transport; service; and precision production/crafts occupations.

The most current revision to the immigration act, which favors the highly skilled workers, those with advanced degrees, and those of exceptional ability is expected to have a positive impact on the occupational profile of immigrants as a whole, and Asian immigrants in particular.

The trends noted above make it likely that underemployment in general is probable among all three immigrant groups. Economic underemployment is expected to be more prevalent among the Vietnamese and Filipinos and less likely among the Indians because of the lower educational background and highly female immigrant stream from these two countries. On the other hand, Indians with their high educational backgrounds and the immigration of professionals recruited from India are expected to experience greater job mismatch and less of the economic forms of underemployment.

3

Data and Methods

The 5% Public Use Microdata Samples (PUMS) of the 1980 and 1990 U.S. Censuses of Population and Housing were used for this study of Asian underemployment since they are the only datasets with sufficient numbers of Asians to make a comparative time study possible. Separate extract data files of working-age respondents for 1980 and 1990 were constructed from the respective 5% PUMS files, ensuring adequate representation of the ethnic groups under consideration. Table 3.1 shows the distribution of the 1980 and 1990 datafiles by ethnicity and, in the case of Asians, national origin. This study was limited to respondents in the usually-defined labor force ages of sixteen through sixty-four at the time the census was taken. It excludes students, retirees, housewives, and those not looking for work.

Table 3.1 Distribution of working age (16–64) respondents in labor force, by ethnic group, 1980 and 1990

Ethnic group	1980			1990		
	Total	Male	Female	Total	Male	Female
Whites	11,180	6,663	4,517	12,375	6,965	5,410
Blacks	8,701	4,484	4,217	9,161	4,520	4,641
Hispanics	12,545	7,574	4,971	19,494	11,749	7,745
Asians						
Japanese	16,695	8,724	7,971	8,920	4,615	4,305
Chinese	16,415	9,171	7,244	15,183	8,124	7,059
Filipino	14,891	7,147	7,744	14,599	6,706	7,893
Korean	6,456	3,029	3,427	6,514	3,144	3,370
Indian	7,700	4,915	2,785	7,314	4,664	2,650
Vietnamese	3,278	1,800	1,478	4,657	2,716	1,941

Determination of the Asian Groups
to Be Studied

While descriptive analyses involve all nine ethnic groups shown in Table 3.1, only three of the six Asian groups will be used for multivariate underemployment modeling. With the goal of identifying the two extreme-ranked Asian groups and one middle-ranked group to be used in testing the explanatory model of underemployment, association modeling (Clogg and Shihadeh 1994) was used to determine the ranks of the nine ethnic groups according to the three variables relevant to the study of underemployment—education, occupation, and nativity. Association modeling involves comparing the distribution of pertinent variables, in this case education, occupation, and nativity, across groups. Row and column scores are assessed and distance between the scores is estimated to determine the rankings of the ethnic groups based on the variable in question. They are subsequently graphed to illustrate the intrinsic association or groupings between the ethnic groups and the pertinent variables.

Figures 3.1–6 show the relative rankings of each of the ethnic groups by education, occupation, and nativity for 1980 and 1990, respectively. As shown in Figure 3.1, the rankings of the ethnic groups by education (highest year of school attended) in 1980 show three distinct clusters: Hispanics, Vietnamese, and blacks at the one extreme; whites, Koreans, and Japanese in the middle group; and Filipinos, Chinese, and Indians, at the other extreme. Actual low-to-high rankings only of the Asian na-

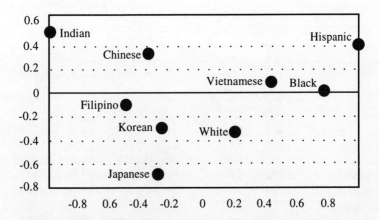

Figure 3.1   Association of ethnic groups by education, 1980

tional origin groups show the following placements: (1) Vietnamese, (2) Koreans, (3) Japanese, (4) Chinese, (5) Filipinos, and (6) Indians. Based on education in 1980 alone, the three Asian group candidates for multivariate modeling are the Vietnamese, the Japanese or Chinese, and the Indians.

Figure 3.2 shows the ranking of ethnic groups by 1980 occupation (U.S. Office of Federal Statistical Policy and Standards 1990). Similar to the education clustering above, the three distinct groupings of ethnic groups by occupation in 1980 are Hispanics, Vietnamese, and blacks at one extreme; whites, Filipinos, Japanese, and Koreans in the middle group; and again, Chinese and Indians at the other extreme. Low-to-high ranking for the Asian national origin groups are as follows: (1) Vietnamese, (2) Japanese, (3) Filipinos, (4) Koreans, (5) Indians, and (6) Chinese. Based on occupation in 1980, Vietnamese, Filipinos or Koreans, and Chinese are the candidates for multivariate modeling.

Rankings based on nativity (years since migration to the United States, or native) in 1980 appear in Figure 3.3. The Asian groups are conspicuously clustered among the recent immigrants, compared to the predominantly native black and white populations. The low-to-high Asian national origin group rankings based on nativity in 1980 are as follows: (1) Vietnamese, (2) Koreans, (3) Indians, (4) Filipinos, (5) Chinese, and (6) Japanese. Candidate Asian groups for multivariate analysis based on nativity in 1980 are thus the Vietnamese, Indians or Filipinos, and the Japanese. Simple averaging of ranks across educa-

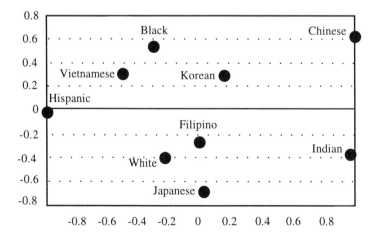

Figure 3.2   Association of ethnic groups by occupation, 1980

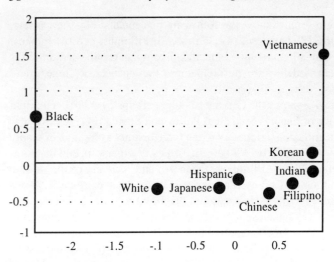

Figure 3.3   Association of ethnic groups by nativity, 1980

tion, occupation, and nativity for 1980 show that Vietnamese, Japanese or Filipinos, and Chinese are the candidates for multivariate modeling.

Following the same procedure as the association modeling performed for 1980, the 1990 results shown in Figures 3.4–6 reveal a rather similar clustering of ethnic groups and a similar set of Asian group finalists for multivariate modeling. The rankings based on education (highest year of school attended) in 1990 (Figure 3.4) show three distinct

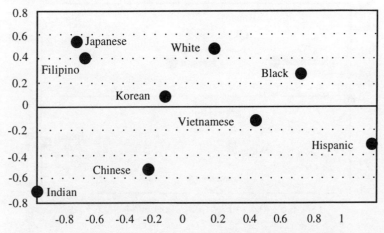

Figure 3.4   Association of ethnic groups by education, 1990

groups; Hispanics, blacks, and Vietnamese make up one group; whites, Koreans, and Chinese form the second group; and Filipinos, Japanese, and Indians make up the last group. Low-to-high Asian group rankings for education in 1990 are as follows: (1) Vietnamese, (2) Korean, (3) Chinese, (4) Filipinos, (5) Japanese, and (6) Indians. Using education in 1990 as the sole criterion, Vietnamese, Chinese or Filipinos, and Indians are the candidate groups for further study.

Figure 3.5 presents the clusters of ethnic groups based on occupation (1990 Standard Occupational Listing) as Hispanics-Vietnamese-blacks, whites-Filipinos-Koreans, and Japanese-Chinese-Indians. The low-to-high ranking of Asian national origin groups based on 1990 occupation is (1) Vietnamese, (2) Filipinos, (3) Koreans, (4) Japanese, (5) Chinese, and (6) Indians. Based on these rankings, the Vietnamese, Koreans or Japanese, and Indians result as the finalists for multivariate analysis.

Finally, the rankings based on nativity (years since immigration to the United States, or native) for 1990 show a lesser degree of clustering among the Asian groups compared to 1980 (Figure 3.6). However, these low-to-high rankings are still indicative of the recent immigration of Asians relative to the black and white populations. The Asian groups are ranked as follows based on nativity in 1990: (1) Vietnamese, (2) Indians, (3) Koreans, (4) Filipinos, (5) Chinese, and (6) Japanese. Candidate groups for modeling analysis based on length of nativity in 1990 are the Vietnamese, Koreans or Filipinos, and the Japanese. Overall

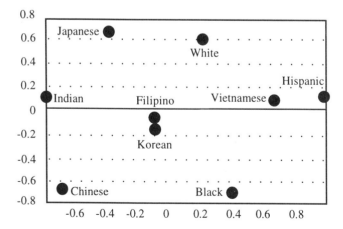

Figure 3.5   Association of ethnic groups by occupation, 1990

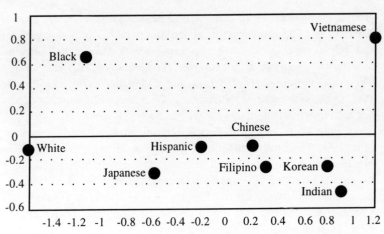

Figure 3.6.   **Association of ethnic groups by nativity, 1990**

rankings of the Asian groups in 1990, based on taking the mean rank across education, occupation, and nativity, show that Vietnamese, Chinese or Filipinos, and Japanese are the groups to be considered for the multivariate modeling of underemployment.

Following the same average ranking procedure used for choosing the candidate Asian groups in 1980 and 1990, a joint rank for both years was calculated. This joint low-to-high ranking is as follows: (1) Vietnamese, (2) Koreans, (3) Filipinos, (4) Japanese, (5) Chinese, and (6) Indians. Consequently, the two extreme immigrant groups—Vietnamese and Indians—and a middle-ranked group—Filipinos—were selected for the multivariate modeling analysis.

Sample Selection Issues

Sample selection occurs when part of a population cannot be studied because of exclusion based on criteria inherent in the choice of the dependent variable (Berk 1983; Winship and Mare 1992). Using the study of underemployment as an example, sample selection occurs because the people who are out of the labor force or who are students have been excluded in the study. In other words, underemployment is assessed only among those who are in the labor force (working or unemployed but looking for work in the four weeks preceeding the census, automatically excluding those out of the labor force).

Correction for sample selection is done by estimating a labor force participation model to determine the odds of being in the labor force or not. Once the labor force participation model is estimated, a value for X_{ij}, which is the logodds of participating in the labor force, is calculated based on the coefficients of the intercepts, the parameter estimates, and the values of X_{ij} for each individual i in group j. The sample selection correction factor is X_{ij}, and it is included in the multivariate analysis of underemployment as an independent variable.

Multivariate Analysis of Labor Force Participation

Labor Force Participation: The Model

The first step in sample selection correction is to estimate the model

$$\lambda_{ij} = \alpha_{ij} + \beta_{ij} *X_{ij} + \varepsilon \qquad \text{Eq. 3.1}$$

where λ_{ij} is the logarithm of the odds that the respondent i in the (gender-year-ethnic) group j was in the labor force, α_{ij} is the intercept for respondent i in group j, β_{ij} is the vector of parameter estimates associated with the vector of independent variables X_{ij} for respondent i in group j, and ε_{ij} is the residual term for respondent i in group j.

Operational Definition of Variables

Correction for sample selection is done using a labor force participation model, where the dependent variable is equal to 1 if the respondent is in the labor force, and equal to 0 if the respondent is out of the labor force or attending school at the time the census was taken. Variables found to be significant predictors of labor force participation, particularly for minority populations (Tienda and Wilson 1992b), are used in the sample selection model. These include United States experience, education, school attendance, presence of a young child in the household, marital status, and age. The operational definitions of these variables are summarized in Table 3.2.

U. S. experience is defined as the number of years since immigration to the United States and is represented in the labor force participation model by the dichotomous variable MIG11PLS, which is equal to 1 if the respondent has been in the United States for eleven years or more, or if the respondent were born in the United States. Labor force participation is expected to increase with more years of U.S. experience.

Table 3.2   Operational definitions of variables used in labor force participation models

Variables	PUMS variables involved		Definition
	1980	1990	
Years in U.S.	IMMIGYR	IMMIGYR	U.S. native, or migrated to U.S. 11 or more years ago (= 1) or not (= 0)
HS graduate +	GRADE FINGRADE	YEARSCH SCHOOL	completed 12 years or more of schooling (= 1) or not (= 0)
School attendance	SCHOOL	SCHOOL	curerently enrolled in school (= 1) or not (= 0)
Child < 6 in HH	CHILDREN	RAGECHLD	presence in household of at least 1 own child under age 6 (= 1) or not (= 0)
Married	MARITAL	MARITAL	now married (except separated) (= 1) or not (= 0)
Age	AGE	AGE	age in years; age in years squared

Education, based on the highest level of school attended, is represented in the sample selection model by the HSPLUS variable. HSPLUS is a dummy variable that is equal to 1 if the respondent finished 12 years of school or more, and equal to 0 if not. Higher education is expected to be positively related to labor force participation.

School attendance is measured from the PUMS variable SCHOOL to capture current school enrollment. It is represented by a dichotomous variable equal to 1 if the respondent is enrolled in school during the time the census was taken, and equal to 0 if not. School attendance is expected to have a negative impact on labor force participation.

Having a young child in the household can reduce participation in the labor force, particularly for women. This is best illustrated by Becker's time allocation theory (1965), which suggests that a person who is caught between family responsibilities (e.g., taking care of a child) and working in a job, will choose the activity that provides the higher personal utility (satisfaction). CHILDHH was formulated to measure this concept, where CHILDHH is equal to 1 if there is a child who is fewer than six years old in the household, or 0 if no such child is residing in the respondent's household. CHILDHH is expected to be negatively related to labor force participation, particularly for women.

Marital status is another family-related determinant of labor force participation, because of its effect in increasing the need for economic resources (brought about by starting a family) and in tied-worker immigration (Sandell 1977). Married men were found to have higher labor force participation rates than unmarried men (Blau and Ferber 1992). However, being married sometimes reduces women's participation in the labor force (Blau and Ferber 1992; Hayghe and Bianchi 1994). Marital status is measured by the MARRIED dichotomous variable which is equal to 1 if married or in a union, and 0 if separated, divorced, or not in a union. The relationship of marital status to labor force participation is unclear and therefore no direction of the relationship is hypothesized.

Age is controlled for in the labor force participation model because of its influence on the major determinants of labor force participation. In particular, it has an impact on migration, school attendance, life course decisions (including work), and family life. It is included in the model as a continuous variable. The squared version of age is also included in the model.

Sample selection models using the variables above are run by gender and year, for each of the four ethnic groups considered for further analysis (whites, Indians, Filipinos, and Vietnamese). A total of sixteen selection equations are estimated—by gender and year, and subsequently incorporated into the multivariate models of underemployment.

Multivariate Analysis of Underemployment

Four levels of underemployment (Clogg 1979; Sullivan 1978) are considered in this study. These are the unemployed, the underemployed based on low hours, the underemployed based on low income, and the underemployed based on job mismatch. The study of underemployment involves simultaneously estimating the logarithm of the odds of being in each of the underemployment categories, relative to being adequately employed.

Underemployment: The Model

The baseline model for this study of underemployment involves a set of human capital, family and household, industry, age, and assimilation variables. Since the study looked at the four forms of underemployment against being adequately employed, correction for sample selection, caused by excluding from the analyses those who were out of the labor force, is incorporated into the models. Polytomous regression models (also called multinomial logit models) (Aldrich and Nelson 1984; Hosmer and Lemeshow 1989) are run, with the following specification:

$$\gamma_{ijk} = \alpha_{ijk} + \beta_{ijk} * X_{ijk} + \lambda_{ijk} + \varepsilon \qquad \text{Eq. 3.2}$$

where γ_{ijk} is the logarithm of the odds of respondent i (i = 1, ..., n) from group j (j = 1, ..., 16) being in a certain underemployment category k (k = 1, ... 4), α_{ijk} is the constant associated with each respondent i from group j in the underemployment category k, β_{ijk} is the parameter estimate associated with the vector of independent variables X_{ijk}, λ_{ijk} is the parameter estimate for selection bias for respondent i from group j in underemployment category k, and ε_{ijk} is the random error term.

Models are run separately by gender, ethnic group (whites, Indians, Filipinos, and Vietnamese), and time (census year). Comparisons between the four ethnic groups with regards to the determinants of the underemployment categories are discussed separately by gender.

Operational Definitions
of Dependent Variables

The four underemployment categories are assessed for nonstudents in the labor force only. An important aspect of the underemployment categories is its hierarchical feature, in which those respondents who are classified in a previous underemployment category are dropped from the pool of those assessed for a succeeding underemployment category. This feature is used to make the underemployment categories mutually exclusive. The underemployment hierarchy is as follows: unemployed, working part-time, working in poverty, job mismatch (and adequately employed) (Clogg 1979; Sullivan 1978).

The unemployed are respondents who were not working but looking for work in the four weeks preceeding the census. This is represented in the model by the dichotomous variable UNEMP which is equal to 1 if unemployed and equal to 0 if not.

Part-time workers are those who worked for thirty-four or fewer hours per week during the four weeks preceeding the census. PARTTIME is equal to 1 if the respondent is working part-time, and equal to 0 if not.

The term *working poor* refers to respondents working at least thirty-five hours per week in the four weeks preceeding the census or those classified as employed but not at work, who reported a previous year individual income below the official poverty level in 1979 and 1989. If the cumulative individual income from salaries, wages, and earnings from self-employment is less than 125 percent of the income threshold cutoff for an unrelated individual (as updated and tabulated by the Social Security Administration),[1] then the respondent is considered to be working in poverty. Entrants and re-entrants to the labor force (those who were working in 1980 or 1990, but did not have income information because they were not working the year before) were not included in the working poverty sort, but were included in the succeeding (mismatch and adequate employment) sorts. WRKPOV is a dummy variable where 1 means that the respondent is working in poverty, and 0 indicates the opposite is true.

Job mismatch measures the extent of "overeducation" of a respondent, relative to the requirements of his/her occupation. The 1980 Occupational Codes were reorganized into homogenous groups based on education, and mismatch cutoff points were determined, based on the mean years of education for a particular occupation, plus one standard deviation (Clogg and Shockey 1984). The mismatch cutoffs calculated by Shihadeh and Clogg (1989) based on the Clogg and Shockey (1984) definitions are used in this study. The same 1980-based cutoffs are used for the 1990 job mismatch measure. A person is considered mismatched if he/she is working at least thirty-five hours a week, not classified in any of the previous underemployment categories, and whose educational attainment is greater than the established cutoff for the occupation that he/she is in. MISMATCH was equal to 1 if the respondent is underemployed by job mismatch, and equal to 0 if not.

The residual category (those not classified into any of the four previous underemployment categories) represents the adequately employed. It is measured by a dummy variable ADEQ, which is equal to 1 if adequately employed and equal to 0 if not.

Operational Definitions of Independent Variables

The independent variables used in the underemployment models are grouped into human capital, family and household, industry, age, and assimilation blocks. The human capital block includes the years of

---

[1]The income cut-offs used in this study were $4717 (a $3774 poverty threshold for unrelated individuals under age sixty-five + 25%) in 1980 and $8064 (a $6451 poverty threshold for unrelated individuals under age sixty-five + 25%) in 1990.

formal education, disability status, and self-employment. Household headship status, number of workers in the family, and the presence of a young child in the household make up the family and household block. The industry block is comprised of dichotomous variables representing the seven major industry groups based on the Standard Industry Codes. Two dummy variables for age, representing the two older age groups, constitute the age block. Recency of migration to the United States and English language ability form the assimilation block of variables. The operational definitions of these variables are summarized in Table 3.3.

Table 3.3   Operational definitions of variables used in underemployment models

Variables	PUMS variables involved		Definition
	1980	*1990*	
Human Capital			
Education	GRADE FINGRADE	YEARSCH SCHOOL	finished <12 years education (LHS); finished 12–15 years formal education (HSSCOL); finished 16 or more years schooling (COLPLUS)
Disability status	DISABIL1	DISABIL1	has work-limiting disability
Self-employment	CLASS	CLASS	self-employed workers (unincorporated business) or employee of own firm
Family and Household			
Householder	RELAT1	RELAT1	household head
No. workers in household	LABOR[a]	RWRKR893	total no. workers in household
Presence of young child in household	CHILDREN	RAGECHILD	presence in household of at least 1 own child < age 6

continued

Table 3.3 continued

	PUMS variables involved		
Variables	*1980*	*1990*	*Definition*
Industry	INDUSTRY	INDUSTRY	employed in manufacturing; agriculture/mining /construction; transportation/communication; trade; business; services; public administration
Assimilation			
Years in U.S.	IMMIGYR	IMMIGYR	migrated to U.S. 10 or fewer years ago; migrated 11 or more years ago;U.S. native-born
English language proficiency	ENGLISH	ENGLISH	speaks only English; speaks English well, very well

Dummy variables coded (= 1); or not (= 0)

ªAssessed for each household member, then summed.

Educational attainment is measured by three dummy variables measuring less than high school (LHS) education, high school graduate plus some college (HSGRAD+SOMECOL), and college graduate or more (COLPLUS). LHS was equal to 1 if the highest level attended by the respondent is fewer than twelve years, and equal to 0 if not. Those who attended twelve to fifteen years of school are considered part of the HSSCOL variable. Respondents who had twelve or more years of schooling, but fewer than sixteen years of education are coded 1 (HSSCOL=1) while those who did not fit this criteria are coded 0. Finally, respondents with sixteen or more years of schooling are classifed as college graduates or more (COLPLUS = 1). The reference category for education is the less- than-high-school category (LHS). It is expected that the economic forms of underemployment, namely unemployment, part-time work, and working poor improves with every level of education completed, and are therefore negatively related. However, education is anticipated to have a positive effect on job mismatch.

The ability to work can be impaired by a disability. Disability status in this study measures only the presence of a work-limiting disability. The presence of a limiting disability may mean lowered chances for getting a full-time job as well as fewer job options available. Although improved handicap access facilities make working possible for disabled workers, employer attitudes, physical incapacity, and physical inaccessibility still keep disabled workers from adequate employment. DISLIM is a dichotomous variable measuring the presence of a limiting disability. It is equal to 1 if the respondent has a limiting disability and equal to 0 if not. Having a limiting disability is expected to be positively related to underemployment.

Self-employment is one way of becoming incorporated into the labor force and is high among the Asians (Tienda and Lii 1987). It can increase the economic forms of underemployment, particularly part-time work and working poor. SELFEMP is defined as a dichotomous variable where 1 equals being self-employed in an unincorporated business or being an employee in one's own corporation, and 0 if not.

Heading a household implies the responsibility of maintaining the household and/or family. Holding a job or being employed is essential to assure the economic well-being of the family. The effect of household head status on underemployment is mixed; it can mean that this responsibility will pressure the individual to get an adequate job, or the same pressure will cause him/her to take on any job available, be it part-time, underpaid, or a job for which the person is overqualified. HHDLR is a dummy variable coded 1 if a household head and coded 0 if not.

The presence of other workers in the family, like the household head situation above, can work both ways. The presence of other earners relieves other family members of the pressure to work. This means that these family members can have more time for job searches thereby remaining unemployed; they can opt for part-time jobs; and, depending on family care situations, they can decide to work in jobs they are overqualified for. NUMWRKR is a continuous variable measuring the actual number of workers in the household.

Similar to the labor force participation model, the presence of a young child in the household may not stop women, in particular, from joining the labor force, but it may keep them from adequate employment. Women may take part-time jobs, mismatched jobs, or unemployment, to incorporate child care responsibilities into their daily routine. CHILDHH is a dummy variable equal to 1 if there is at least one child in the household who is six years old or under, and equal to 0 if there is none. The presence of a young child in the household is expected to increase the likelihood of being underemployed, particularly for women.

Industry has impacts on underemployment depending on the type of industry in which a worker is incorporated. In some industries, like service (Sheets et al. 1987) and trade, low wages and part-time work are common. Unemployment is prevalent for those in manufacturing, following its decline. White-collar occupations in transportation and communication and in business have greater chances of job mismatch. As a result, the influence of industry on underemployment is determined by the worker's specific type of industry. Industry is composed of a set of seven dummy variables each representing membership in either agriculture/mining/construction, manufacturing, transportation and communication, trade, business, service, and public administration (= 1) or not (= 0).

Age is included in the model as a control variable. Previous research shows that underemployment is more likely among the young and adequacy of employment improves as one ages (Clogg and Sullivan 1983). Age is included in the model as a series of dummy variables. YOUNG, representing those aged sixteen to thirty (= 1) or not (= 0), MIDAGE, representing those aged thirty-one to forty-five (= 1) or not (= 0), or OLD, representing those aged forty-six to sixty-four (= 1) or not (= 0). A negative association between age and underemployment is expected.

Nativity is measured by three dummy variables representing different subsets of years of U.S. experience. MIG10 is a dummy variable equal to 1 if the respondent immigrated to the U.S. in the last ten years, and equal to 0 if not. MIG11+ is equal to 1 if the respondent immigrated to the U.S. eleven or more years prior to the census year, and equal to 0 if not. The U.S.-born (NATIVE = 1) respondents comprised the reference group. The labor force literature leads us to expect a negative relationship between years of U.S. experience and underemployment. Recent migrants are expected to be disadvantaged in the labor force at least in the short term, and are therefore expected to be more likely to experience underemployment than older migrants and native workers.

Part of the general disadvantage of recent migrants in the labor force is their English language proficiency. Those who are not fluent in the language often have to settle for jobs where communication is not critical—often low-wage, manual jobs. Underemployment is therefore expected to be more likely among those who are not fluent in the English language. English language proficiency is operationalized as a dichotomous variable which indicates the language spoken at home. The measure for English proficiency is based on answers to a fluency question, where answers are categorized into a four-point scale of English language fluency. A dummy variable (FLUENT) where 1 is equal to English fluency ("good" and speaks "very well") and 0 was equal to non-proficiency ("fair" and "poor") is included in the model.

This chapter has outlined the data used for this study, the plan for statistical analysis, as well as the operational definitions of the variables used in the models. The results of the labor force participation (sample selection) analysis are discussed in Chapter 5, while the multivariate analysis of underemployment discussion starts in Chapter 6.

4

A Descriptive Profile of Asian Underemployment in the United States

Assessing Asian immigrant underemployment as an indicator of economic assimilation is best measured relative to the white majority. This methodology places the Asian groups in a comparative perspective with the most integrated ethnic group in the United States labor market. Using a sample of immigrant and native workers in the civilian labor force, the descriptive analysis in this chapter starts with an overall appraisal of the underemployment trends by ethnic group, for 1980 and 1990. The analysis is then disaggregated by gender, reflecting differential underemployment trends during the 10-year time span, between men and women. Finally, underemployment trends are analyzed by ethnic group and categories of selected independent variables.

The independent variables presented in this chapter reflect factors that are believed to have an impact on underemployment, a relationship that is tested in Chapter 6. Education improves the economic situation of workers through better jobs and wages. The percentage of people experiencing the economic forms of underemployment (unemployed, part-time work, and working poor) ia expected to decrease with increasing years of education. However, job mismatch is common among the highly educated and is therefore expected to be high among this group relative to those with less education. Nativity affects underemployment in that migrants usually face at least temporary disadvantage in the labor force. Native-born workers are therefore expected to suffer less underemployment than migrants, with the percentage of migrants who are underemployed expected to decrease with increased duration in the United States. Underemployment is expected to be highest among the youngest group of workers, while improving for the older age groups. The percentage of underemployment by household type is expected to reveal the disadvantaged situation among women heads of households, particularly on forms of economic underemployment. The industrial sector has different impacts on underemployment, depending on the industry of incorporation. Trade and service industries are expected to have high percentages of underemployment, particularly economic underemployment.

Asian Underemployment Trends and Differentials

Total underemployment is highest among Indians in 1980 at 50 percent and lowest among non-Hispanic whites at 36 percent (Figure 4.1). This pattern is replicated in 1990, with the Indian total underemployment rate down to 47 percent while the non-Hispanic white and Vietnamese groups have 1990 underemployment rates around 35 percent. Between 1980 and 1990, all three Asian groups exhibited reductions in overall underemployment, with Filipinos showing the greatest reduction at 9 percent. It is interesting to note that the underemployment rate for non-Hispanic whites barely changed between 1980 and 1990.

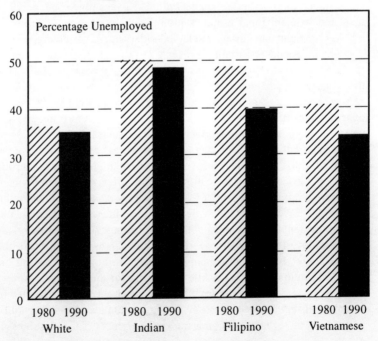

Figure 4.1   Total underemployment by ethnic group, year

The distribution of the different underemployment components as a factor of total underemployment varies across ethnic groups (Figure 4.2). Unemployment is highest among the Vietnamese and lowest for Filipinos in 1980 and 1990. For the same years, part-time employment is highest among non-Hispanic whites and lowest among Indians. Vietnamese have the highest rates of working poverty among the ethnic groups considered during the same years. Over 25 percent of Indians are mismatched in 1980 and 1990, representing the highest job mismatch rate among the ethnic groups. The job mismatch rates for Indians and Filipinos are more than double those of the non-Hispanic whites and Vietnamese. Finally, 65 percent of the non-Hispanic whites are adequately employed compared to only 50 percent among Indians.

There are distinct dynamics in underemployment patterns across groups and across time. For example, there is generally a decreasing

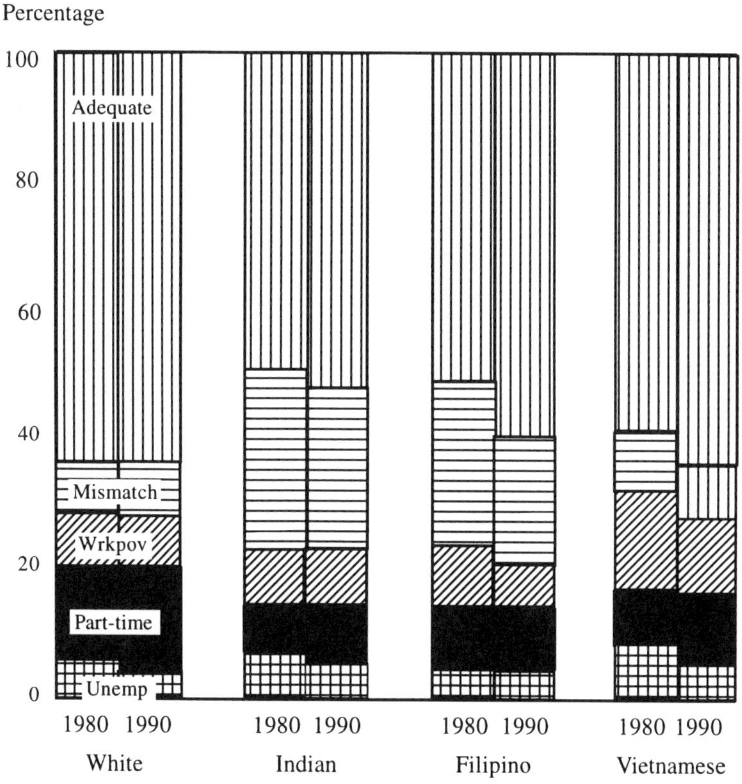

Figure 4.2   Underemployment by ethnic group, year

trend in unemployment observed. Part-time employment is on the rise, as reflected by increases among whites, Indians, and Vietnamese between 1980 and 1990. The pattern for working poverty between 1980 and 1990 is generally downward. Job mismatch is generally decreasing across groups, except for whites. Finally, adequate employment increased for most groups, except for whites. In sum, the pervading pattern between 1980 and 1990 considering all the groups is a decrease in unemployment, an increase in part-time employment, a decrease in working poverty and job mismatch, and an increase in adequate employment.

The discussion above effectively paints the general picture of underemployment across ethnic groups in the United States. However, it masks the magnitude of differences across groups in the percentage of people in each underemployment category. Furthermore, the underemployment category that holds the greatest percentage of the people for each group also varies. For example, working part-time had the highest proportion (15 percent) of whites compared to any other underemployment category. Mismatch was the predominant category for two Asian groups, with close to one-third for Indians and one-fifth for Filipinos. Vietnamese are represented significantly in the disadvantaged underemployed categories of unemployed, part-time employed, and working poor. Easily deduced from the above is the predominant experience of mismatch among the Asian groups except for the Vietnamese, and the significant experience of part-time work among whites. Also notable is the moderate proportion of Vietnamese in the unemployed and working poor categories.

Gender Differences
in Asian Underemployment

The disaggregated analysis by gender presents another facet of the dynamics in the underemployment experience of each ethnic group considered in this study. There is considerable variation in underemployment measures and overall underemployment trends in each underemployment category for men and women.

Gender differentials in total underemployment are shown in Figure 4.3. In 1980, Indian women had the highest level of total underemployment at 50 percent, compared to non-Hispanic white and Vietnamese women at 45 percent. The Indian women remain as the group with the highest total underemployment rate in 1990, with non-Hispanic white women having the lowest total underemployment rate. On the other hand, total underemployment among men in 1980 ranged from a high of 49

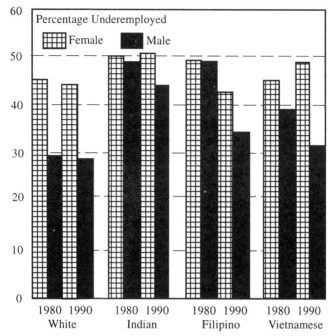

Figure 4.3   Total underemployment by ethnic group, year, gender

percent among Indians to a low of 29 percent for non-Hispanic whites. The patterns for 1990 repeat the groups with the highest and lowest total underemployment percentages.

In all ethnic groups and both years, total underemployment of women is higher than that of men. Gender differences in overall underemployment in 1980 show that non-Hispanic whites exhibited the greatest gender differential, at 16 percent. In contrast, Filipinos displayed minimal disparities in total underemployment, with less than a percentage difference between the two gender groups. In 1990, the non-Hispanic whites remain as the group with the highest percentage difference in total underemployment between men and women, with the differential increasing to 17 percent. However, the lowest differential in total underemployment rate between men and women in 1990 is found among the Indians (8 percent). While the disparity in underemployment by gender barely increased for non-Hispanic whites, all of the three Asian groups experienced an increase in the female-male total underemployment rates with significant increases in gender disparity seen for Filipinos (8 percent) and for Vietnamese (10 percent).

The following discussion of underemployment by category is based on Figures 4.4 and 4.5 for category-specific women's and men's underemployment, respectively. Indian and Vietnamese women have a high of 9 percent unemployment in 1980 compared to Filipino women at 5 percent. Corresponding figures for men in 1980 are a high of 8 percent for Vietnamese and a low of 4 percent for Indians and Filipinos. For 1990 unemployment, the figures are somewhat similar: a high of 7 percent for Vietnamese women and a low of 4 percent for non-Hispanic white and Filipino women, while men reflected a high of 7 percent for Vietnamese and a low of 4 percent for Indians and Filipinos.

Part-time employment for women in 1980 is highest for whites at 24 percent and lowest for Filipinos and Vietnamese at 14 percent each. For men, part-time employment in 1980 is highest among non-Hispanic

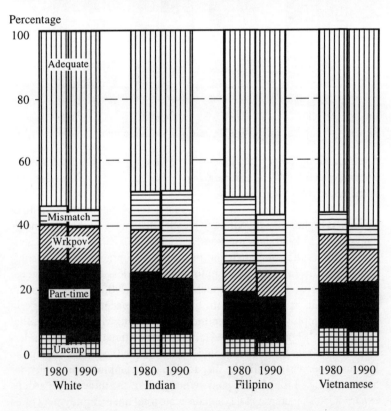

Figure 4.4   Distribution of women's employment status by ethnic group, year

Percentage

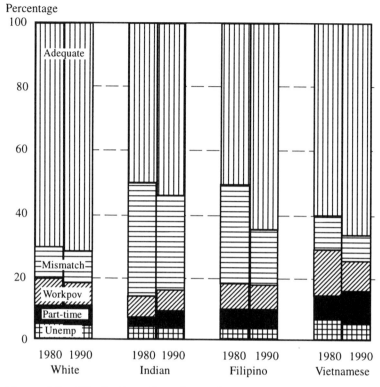

Figure 4.5   Disribution of men's employment status by ethnic group, year

whites at 7 percent and lowest among Indians at 4 percent. The trend for part-time employment in 1990 remains the same for women, with whites having the highest percentage (25) and Filipinos the lowest (13). Part-time employment among men in 1990 show a high of 9 percent among Vietnamese and a low of 5 percent among Indians.

The percentage of women in working poverty was highest among Vietnamese women (16 percent) and lowest among Filipino women (10 percent) in 1980. The corresponding trend for men shows the Vietnamese to have the highest percentage of working poor (13 percent) with non-Hispanic whites and Indians at the low end (6 percent). Vietnamese women remain with the highest working poor rate among the women in 1990 at 11 percent, with Filipinos down to 8 percent. For men, working poverty in 1990 is still highest among Vietnamese at 8 percent, with the rest of the male groups showing similar 1990 working poor rates of about 6 percent. The trend generally shows a decrease in working poor between 1980 and 1990 for both genders. Vietnamese men and women showed the greatest decrease in working poor between 1980 and 1990, at 5 percent each.

Job mismatch is highest among Filipino women in 1980 (20 percent) and lowest among non-Hispanic white women (4 percent). For men, the corresponding figures are a high of 35 percent among Indians, and a low of 11 percent among non-Hispanic whites and Vietnamese. In 1990, the groups at the high and low end of job mismatch remain the same with 18 percent of Filipino women and 5 percent of non-Hispanic white women mismatched in 1990. Indian men who are mismatched is down to 29 percent in 1990 while non-Hispanic white and Vietnamese male job mismatch is down to 9 percent. The trend in job mismatch between 1980 and 1990 generally shows an increase among women (except for Filipinos) and a decrease among men. Filipino men show the greatest decrease in job mismatch between 1980 and 1990, with an almost 13 percent reduction compared to single-digit reductions for the rest of the male ethnic groups.

Vietnamese women were the most adequately employed in 1980 at 57 percent, compared to a low of 48 percent adequately employed for Indian women. Adequate employment for men in 1980 is highest among non-Hispanic whites at 71 percent and lowest for Indians at 51 percent. The 1990 figures show the same trend for women, with Vietnamese adequate employment at 61 percent and Indians at 48 percent. For men, the 1990 figures show non-Hispanic white adequate employment rising to 72 percent, and Indian adequate employment also rising to 56 percent.

The overall underemployment trend between 1980 and 1990 by gender shows a decrease in unemployment for all groups (but one) regardless of gender. However, the female unemployment rate remains slightly higher than that of males across ethnic groups (except for non-Hispanic whites and Filipinos in 1990). Except for Filipino males and females, all the other groups exhibited a slight increase in part-time employment between 1980 and 1990, regardless of gender. Working poverty decreased as well between 1980 and 1990 for seven of the eight gender-ethnic groups. Indian males are the only exception, where working poverty increased slightly between 1980 and 1990. Job mismatch has increased for all but one group of women (Filipinos), and decreased for all groups of men. Finally, adequate employment has generally increased except for Indian women.

What is the dominant form of underemployment of each ethnic group represented? White women are overrepresented in the part-time employed category for both years, while white men are more likely to be in the mismatched category. Indian women are either employed part-time or mismatched, while the Indian men are highly mismatched. Filipinos are mostly mismatched. The majority of the Vietnamese women are either working part-time or working poor, while Vietnamese men are more or less equally divided among being employed part-time, working poor, or being mismatched.

In summary, this gender analysis reflects the differences in underemployment experiences by gender and ethnic group, which is concealed in the general trend analysis reported earlier in this chapter. Women across the ethnic groups are over-represented in the part-time employment category, except for Filipino women who were mostly mismatched and Vietnamese women who were also working poor. The men are best characterized as experiencing job mismatch, except for Vietnamese men who are also employed part-time and working poor.

Asian Underemployment by Selected Characteristics

Now that we have looked at general and gender-specific underemployment trends, let us look at underemployment trends across categories of selected independent variables considered to be important determinants of underemployment. Underemployment by type is examined across educational attainment, nativity, age, household type, and industry categories between 1980 and 1990.

Educational Attainment

Table 4.1 shows the distribution of underemployment by ethnicity and educational attainment. Striking, but not unexpected, is the decreasing percentage of disadvantaged underemployed (unemployed, part-time employed, and working poor) as one progresses across increasing educational attainment categories. Indeed, the rates of disadvantaged underemployed decreased with increases in educational attainment. In contrast, rates of job mismatch increased with educational attainment.

Non-Hispanic whites who had a high school education or less showed the highest percentages of part-time employment (at around 16 percent). Those with some college and college graduates revealed increasing job mismatch rates with part-time employment percentages still above 10 percent. Finally, over one-third of non-Hispanic whites with a

Table 4.1   **Distribution of underemployment[a] by educational attainment, ethnicity, year**

Under-employment category	\<HS 1980	1990	HS graduate 1980	1990	Some college 1980	1990	College graduate 1980	1990	Postcollege 1980	1990
White										
Unemployed	10.32	11.44	6.15	5.50	4.41	2.37	2.07	2.37	0.52	0.96
Working P-T	16.63	17.19	14.72	16.13	14.51	12.69	10.54	12.69	8.40	12.34
Working poor	10.00	12.17	9.02	9.30	6.32	4.70	5.43	4.70	1.57	2.70
Job mismatch	0.56	0.32	1.73	1.28	7.01	21.26	23.22	21.26	37.53	33.17
Asian Indian										
Unemployed	11.80	10.21	8.47	6.04	8.34	5.74	6.30	4.36	2.17	3.26
Working P-T	10.96	13.67	10.42	10.31	11.31	11.11	8.51	10.63	5.35	6.52
Working poor	14.54	16.80	10.32	14.48	11.20	8.52	10.45	6.83	3.13	3.34
Job mismatch	0.11	2.31	0.49	2.14	11.42	4.63	27.20	33.30	52.53	42.66
Filipino										
Unemployed	8.09	9.24	5.33	5.75	4.08	3.42	2.43	3.03	1.45	2.08
Working P-T	14.51	15.3	12.56	12.95	9.48	8.38	8.35	7.90	7.24	10.41
Working poor	12.87	13.3	10.30	11.17	9.16	6.81	7.17	5.15	3.41	3.44
Job mismatch	4.45	0.50	11.14	1.95	23.08	4.37	37.83	35.48	43.54	48.24
Vietnamese										
Unemployed	11.10	12.73	8.63	7.30	5.66	4.74	5.52	2.85	1.72	1.36
Working P-T	13.26	15.53	9.55	12.25	7.32	10.36	4.48	6.34	9.48	4.07
Working poor	16.84	11.57	14.84	11.56	12.98	7.15	8.62	6.50	5.17	1.81
Job mismatch	0.09	0.48	0.09	1.58	12.31	4.10	40.69	26.78	51.72	43.44

[a] Residual percentage for each cell reflects distribution of the adequately employed.

post-college education are predominantly mismatched in their jobs.

Indians with less than a high school education had the greatest representation among the working poor. High school graduates and those with some college have equal representation among the part-time employed and the working poor, at around 10 to 12 percent. Job mismatch percentages starts to increase among those with some college, but it becomes the predominant underemployment category among college graduate and postcollege-educated Indians.

Filipinos with a high school education or less are equally distributed between the part-time employed and the working poor. The distribution of underemployment among Filipinos with some college education ran across most of the underemployment categories. The distribution becomes significantly skewed towards the job mismatched as over 35 percent of Filipino college graduates and over 44 percent of post-college educated Filipinos are mismatched.

One finding that this table shows is that controlling for level of education, the Vietnamese show trends similar to the other ethnic groups. Vietnamese with less than a high school education, high school graduation, or some college are predominantly working part-time or working poor. On the other hand, Vietnamese who are college graduates or have a postcollege education are predominantly job mismatched.

What is manifested in the analysis of underemployment by educational attainment is the predominance of marginal employment (unemployment, part-time work, and working in poverty) among the lower educational categories, and the predominance of job mismatch among those in the higher educational categories. Job mismatch is most prevalent among those who had postcollege education, where the proportion mismatched is close to 50 percent. These results are consistent with previous research (Clifford Clogg and Edward Shihadeh [Department of Sociology, Louisiana State University], unpublished data) which finds that job mismatch is commonplace among highly educated individuals, while marginal employment is common among the less educated.

Nativity

Prior research in economic assimilation suggest an initial disadvantage of immigrants in employment in the U.S. labor market (Borjas 1986; Chiswick 1986; Jiobu, 1990), which is examined particularly in Table 4.2. Each of the underemployment categories was analyzed based on the proportion of people in each ethnic group that falls into the specific nativity categories ranging from being a recent migrant (migrated less than or equal to five years ago) to being born in the United States. Non-

Table 4.2 Distribution of underemployment[a] by migration status, ethnicity, year

Under-employment category	Migrated								U.S. born	
	≤ 5 yrs		6–10 yrs		11–15 yrs		16+ yrs			
	1980	1990	1980	1990	1980	1990	1980	1990	1980	1990
White										
Unemployed	11.76	11.90	8.51	6.52	8.16	5.77	5.79	2.74	5.74	4.79
Working P-T	5.88	7.14	12.77	8.70	14.29	17.31	18.60	18.49	14.05	15.14
Working poor	7.84	16.67	6.38	4.35	10.20	7.69	4.96	5.14	7.91	7.64
Job mismatch	25.49	16.67	17.02	30.43	8.16	19.23	9.09	8.56	7.83	7.35
Asian Indian										
Unemployed	9.16	8.31	4.50	4.60	3.29	3.27	3.23	3.72	7.23	6.90
Working P-T	7.20	10.88	7.51	8.06	6.25	9.33	8.23	9.14	17.82	13.79
Working poor	13.63	15.58	5.74	8.40	3.29	6.06	4.03	3.06	9.24	8.62
Job mismatch	20.98	20.61	30.36	25.72	40.46	25.07	37.10	28.82	11.26	12.07
Filipino										
Unemployed	5.56	6.32	3.27	3.59	2.47	3.48	3.51	3.28	5.95	4.82
Working P-T	9.56	10.24	8.96	8.45	10.33	9.51	11.91	9.50	13.06	13.06
Working poor	16.23	15.50	5.79	7.28	4.83	5.18	4.41	4.26	9.83	6.64
Job mismatch	28.65	21.49	30.44	22.56	28.35	18.17	21.05	16.31	10.80	8.76
Vietnamese										
Unemployed	8.68	13.23	6.43	7.36	8.86	4.60	3.33	4.12	3.39	9.68
Working P-T	8.87	14.83	17.14	11.61	11.39	9.04	13.33	14.71	13.56	9.68
Working poor	14.17	14.97	14.64	10.23	11.39	6.08	6.67	7.65	13.56	17.74
Job mismatch	8.47	3.63	5.71	6.76	18.99	8.82	23.33	11.18	13.56	11.29

[a]Residual percentage for each cell reflects distribution of the adequately employed.

Hispanic whites and Filipinos followed the assimilation pathway with the most recent migrants showing the highest underemployment rate, steadily decreasing among the earlier migrant categories, culminating with the native-born showing the lowest underemployment rate.

Unemployment was highest among the recent immigrants for all groups and it steadily decreased with increased duration in the United States. However, it was interesting to find that unemployment was actually higher among the native-born of all ethnic groups compared to all but the recent migrant groups—a result that is stronger in 1990. Results show increasing part-time employment rates for non-Hispanic whites with earlier migrants showing a higher percentage of part-time employment compared to more recent migrants, with U.S.-born rates somewhere in the middle of the range. In contrast, U.S.-born Indians and Filipinos show the highest percentage of part-time employment compared to any of the migrant categories. Overall, part-time employment rates are highest among the non-Hispanic whites.

Recent Asian migrants start out with the highest percentages of working poverty, something which became evident for non-Hispanic whites as well in 1990. Working poverty rates then tend to decrease with duration of stay in the U.S., but increases again for the U.S.-born. In fact, the native-born of all four ethnic groups exhibited the second highest (after recent migrants) percentages of working poor.

Job mismatch rates were high for most of the migrant groups. Native-born non-Hispanic whites, Indians, and Filipinos have the lowest job mismatch rates compared to the other migrant categories. In contrast, recent Vietnamese migrants showed the lowest percentage of job mismatch with the highest rates among the earliest migrants (16 years or more) and the native-born Vietnamese. Within ethnic group variations in underemployment by nativity are apparent in the tables.

Whites show the highest proportion of adequate employment among those born in the United States, and the most recent migrants have the lowest percentage of being adequately employed. At the same time, the most recent migrants also have high proportions of mismatch and unemployment. Scrutiny of the 1990 figures reveals that the most recent migrants still had the lowest percentage of being adequately employed, and the highest proportion of the unemployed. Part-time employment is highest among the older two migrant groups. Curiously, job mismatch is highest among those who migrated between six and ten years, and lowest among the native-born.

Underemployment trends for Indians show an interesting deviation from the assimilation path. In 1980, the lowest percentage of adequately employed Indians can be found among the two older migrant groups, which also have the highest prevalence of mismatch. At the same time, mismatch was significantly higher in all migrant groups compared to those born in the United States. This may reflect the stock of migrants coming from India in the 1960s, who (see Chapter 2) are mostly occupational preference migrants. Consistent with the findings for whites, unemployment among Indians is highest among the most recent arrivals. Figures for Indians in 1990 show trends more consistent with the assimilation path. The percentage adequately employed is lowest among the most recent migrants and highest among the native-born. Job mismatch is still considerably higher across all migrant groups compared to those born in the United States. Marginal employment (unemployment and working poverty) is also highest among the most recent migrants.

Assessing the percentage that is adequately employed shows that Filipinos follow the traditional assimilation path for both years. The proportion adequately employed is lowest among the most recent migrants and highest among the native-born Filipinos in 1980 and 1990. Job mismatch in both years is highest among the two more recent migrant groups compared to the two older ones, but migrant mismatch is still significantly higher than native-born job mismatch. Unemployment in both years is highest among the most recent migrants and the native-born Filipinos.

The Vietnamese underemployment trend exhibits their manner of immigration to the United States. In 1980, adequate employment was lowest among the two older migrant groups, primarily because of high mismatch figures. These cover prewar migrants who were mostly professionals (Rutledge 1992). Figures for 1990 show the native-born as the least adequately employed, followed by the most recent migrants. Significant is the finding that marginal employment was highest among the most recent migrants, reflecting their refugee status. Job mismatch is lowest among the most recent migrants and highest among the native-born, possibly from difficulties in economic assimilation usually faced by a minority group that is generally new to the United States.

Although specific underemployment patterns by nativity vary across ethnic groups, some similarities exist. There is a progressive improvement in adequate employment across nativity categories in two ethnic groups, but the advantage of the native-born group is illustrated in three of the four groups, for both years. Unemployment is highest in 1980 and 1990 among the most recent migrants in all ethnic groups studied. Finally, marginal employment is high among the most recent migrants. Explanations for these trends cover the migrant economic disadvantage thesis and the assimilation perspective, which theorize about the difficulty of economic assimilation among migrants because they lack location-specific capital (DaVanzo 1981). Also important are status at the time of immigration, historical/political events (for Vietnamese refugees), and changes in U.S. immigration policy.

Age

Age effects in employment are evident in the two extreme age groups—the 16–25 year olds and the 56–65 year olds (see Table 4.3). As expected, the youngest age group experienced the least adequate employment in each year. Since marginal employment is typical in the employment experience of younger workers, this result is not surprising. In fact, for all of the ethnic groups, unemployment and working poverty are highest among those aged 16–25 in 1980 and 1990. This result reflects the difficulties in the school-to-job transitions common in this age group. Part-time employment in both years is common among the oldest age group of all the ethnic groups considered, although it was also high for Filipinos and Vietnamese in the 16–25 year age group. Job mismatch is usually spread out across the middle age groups, indicative of the selective occurrence of mismatch among higher positions, which are usually occupied by older (longer tenured) workers.

Specific age patterns of underemployment across the different ethnic groups are not as varied as those of education or nativity. Across both time frames, younger whites compared to all other age groups experience the least adequate employment, and the most unemployment and working poverty. On the other hand, most of the part-time employment of whites is among the 56–64 age group. Except for the youngest white workers, a pattern of increasing job mismatch is observed between 1980 and 1990.

A similar situation of low adequate employment, high unemployment, and high working poverty is shown for 16–25 year-old Indians in 1980 and 1990. At the same time, the trend for adequate employment improves progressively across age groups for Indians. More younger workers are employed part-time in 1980 while older (56–64) part-time workers are prevalent in 1990.

Filipinos consistently show low adequate employment, high unemployment, and high working poverty for workers aged 16–25, as well as the higher prevalence of part-time work among the 56–65 year olds. Mismatch is most prevalent among the middle age groups. For Filipinos, these same patterns are observed for 1980 and 1990.

Table 4.3　Distribution of underemployment[a] by age, ethnicity, and year

Under-employment category	16–25 years		26–35 years		36–45 years		45–55 years		56–64 years	
	1980	1990	1980	1990	1980	1990	1980	1990	1980	1990
White										
Unemployed	21.01	8.88	10.91	4.82	6.85	3.97	6.45	3.91	5.97	3.26
Working P-T	12.68	14.77	11.48	14.73	13.98	14.75	15.88	13.25	21.22	22.02
Working poor	19.38	17.63	9.42	6.48	7.65	5.79	8.46	5.86	8.39	6.12
Job mismatch	7.86	4.72	7.59	7.87	5.64	9.01	2.89	7.69	3.18	6.04
Asian Indian										
Unemployed	11.82	8.36	6.30	4.79	3.69	3.86	7.38	5.06	5.53	6.70
Working P-T	9.26	13.65	8.01	9.35	6.75	9.47	9.47	7.29	14.89	10.99
Working poor	19.66	18.43	8.42	9.97	4.83	5.45	7.26	4.25	11.06	7.77
Job mismatch	14.96	8.36	29.53	23.88	32.44	28.86	22.26	28.49	11.06	20.64
Filipino										
Unemployed	6.82	8.61	4.00	3.40	2.68	2.93	4.41	3.70	5.62	5.90
Working P-T	12.41	13.69	9.91	8.56	9.98	9.36	9.38	8.70	13.58	13.82
Working poor	18.79	16.87	7.93	7.10	5.41	5.10	6.75	5.55	9.60	8.31
Job mismatch	15.25	8.08	28.24	17.12	29.86	21.43	21.58	20.92	14.52	13.51
Vietnamese										
Unemployed	10.59	11.01	7.53	5.97	5.51	6.19	9.55	6.18	17.54	8.63
Working P-T	11.14	13.95	9.00	9.26	10.43	11.06	7.96	13.63	11.40	12.69
Working poor	19.39	17.33	13.43	7.74	9.86	7.86	15.29	7.45	9.65	8.63
Job mismatch	3.99	4.99	10.18	6.70	10.00	9.05	9.24	8.87	12.28	7.11

[a]Residual percentage for each cell reflects distribution of the adequately employed.

No consistent age pattern in underemployment is apparent for the Vietnamese, except that job mismatch is usually higher in the older age groups than in the younger ones. Evident from the discussion of age patterns in underemployment is one general conclusion: the disadvantage of younger workers in the labor force, as proven by higher levels of unemployment and working poverty, and lower levels of adequate employment across ethnic groups and over time.

Household Type

Various studies have documented the role of family situations on employment. One general consensus is the role that children play in the employment decisions of the parents. The presence of younger children is usually detrimental to the employment situation of the mother in a married couple household, or in a female-headed household. Marital status is also an important determinant given that women in a married couple household are more likely to be employed (either full-time or part-time) than women in female-headed households. The patterns of underemployment reflect these views.

Whites and Filipinos living in female-headed households have lower measures of adequate employment compared to the other household types (see Table 4.4). A high percentage of working poverty is also perceptible for all ethnic groups among female-headed households. Job mismatch for both years is highest for people in nonfamily households for all of the ethnic groups. This mismatch may be indicative of two things: the relatively young age of white-collar workers or the demands of white-collar work prompting these workers to delay family formation. Ethnic variations in the patterns of underemployment by household type exist, although the trend of female-headed household disadvantage is a pervading theme. Whites show consistent trends of low adequate employment and high unemployment among such households in each year. Given the same time frame, job mismatch was also consistently highest in whites in nonfamily households. Unlike whites, adequate employment among Indians is lowest among those in households headed by men across time. Consistent findings for 1980 and 1990 also show the following results for Indians: highest unemployment and part-time employment among female-headed households, highest working poverty among the households headed by men, and job mismatch highest among nonfamily households. Lowest adequate employment for Filipinos in both years is evident among the female-headed households. However, a higher prevalence of unemployment and working poverty is occurring

Table 4.4   Distribution of underemployment^a by household
type, ethnicity, year

Underemployment category	Married couple		Male householder		Female householder		Nonfamily household	
	1980	1990	1980	1990	1980	1990	1980	1990
White								
Unemployed	5.40	4.11	5.81	7.16	9.26	8.37	5.92	4.12
Working P-T	14.86	16.14	15.35	9.98	13.45	14.80	10.57	12.00
Working poor	7.38	7.31	7.88	9.98	13.32	9.67	6.59	5.22
Job mismatch	7.30	8.01	7.47	8.92	3.68	6.67	10.97	10.90
Asian Indian								
Unemployed	6.09	4.69	8.60	6.43	10.90	7.54	3.75	4.35
Working P-T	8.10	9.69	6.45	6.96	9.48	11.51	7.88	6.21
Working poor	7.92	7.15	14.52	14.78	12.32	9.92	7.63	5.28
Job mismatch	27.93	25.72	22.58	21.57	13.27	12.70	31.54	30.12
Filipino								
Unemployed	4.29	3.94	6.21	5.51	4.49	5.29	3.58	3.35
Working P-T	10.80	10.29	6.56	8.61	11.95	10.10	9.11	6.30
Working poor	8.00	7.11	14.52	9.57	11.95	8.02	9.34	4.92
Job mismatch	24.64	17.72	22.58	14.70	21.86	18.56	21.06	20.67
Vietnamese								
Unemployed	7.95	6.36	10.18	8.50	12.62	9.43	5.90	4.32
Working P-T	9.28	11.31	10.55	10.03	12.29	14.25	9.83	7.91
Working poor	13.02	8.27	15.64	11.42	19.60	12.94	13.76	5.76
Job mismatch	9.55	7.47	6.91	6.27	5.65	6.36	7.30	15.11

^aResidual percentage for each cell reflects distribution of the adequately

among households headed by men. Part-time employment is highest
among female-headed households and job mismatch is evenly distributed across household type. Patterns of underemployment by household
type are consistent for the Vietnamese in both years. Women's disadvantage is most apparent from the Vietnamese results, as shown by female-headed households having the highest proportion of unemployed,
part-time workers, working poor, and a low percentage of adequate employment. Like the whites, Vietnamese in nonfamily households experience the greatest percentage of job mismatch. The predominant pattern
of underemployment by household type is one of disadvantage among
female-headed households. This is apparent in almost all ethnic groups
and consistent across time. Nonmarital pregnancy, childrearing versus
work conflicts, and economic drawbacks for women from marital dissolution are all plausible explanations for the economic disadvantage of
female-headed households. A surprising finding is the high marginal
employment in households headed by Indian and Filipino men. It is

speculated that the changing make-up of the labor market is partly responsible, and that perhaps the jobs that these men were originally in are jobs that are being abolished in the changing labor market.

Industry

In light of the changing economy from predominantly goods-producing to predominantly service-producing, the concentration of one group in a particular industrial sector has significant effects on the underemployment situation of these ethnic groups. The ethnic groups who are disproportionately represented in one of the goods-producing sectors ultimately suffer, while those concentrated in the service-producing sector benefit from the changing labor market situation.

Table 4.5 shows the underemployment distribution by ethnicity and industry. General 1980 and 1990 trends show the highest percentage of unemployment in the agricultural, mining, and construction industries for all ethnic groups. Part-time employment for the same years is high in the service and trade industries, and working poverty is highest in the trade industry. Job mismatch is highest in public administration for whites and Indians and in business for Filipinos and Vietnamese. Finally, adequate employment is lowest in the trade industry in 1980 and 1990.

It appears therefore that while patterns are not as consistent across time and across ethnic groups as they were for the earlier variables considered, marginal employment seems more typical in trade. Whites have consistent underemployment measures for unemployment, part-time employment, working poor, and job mismatch. Unemployment is highest in agriculture, part-time employment in service, working poverty in trade, and job mismatch in public administration. Indian underemployment trends by industry show consistently high unemployment over time in the agricultural sector, high part-time employment and working poverty as well as low adequate employment in the trade industry. Filipinos reflect similar underemployment patterns, with unemployment highest in agriculture, part-time employment and working poverty highest in trade, and low adequate employment also in trade. Results of the underemployment analysis for the Vietnamese do not reveal any consistent findings across time, except for the high percentage of unemployment in the agricultural industry.

While the results of this section are not as consistent as the other variables, the predominance of unemployment in agriculture, mining, and construction, together with marginal employment in trade is worth noting. Job mismatch is also increasingly found as highest in the public

Table 4.5 Distribution of underemployment[a] by industry, ethnicity, year

Underemployment Category	Agriculture/mining /construction 1980	1990	Manufacturing 1980	1990	Transportation/ communications 1980	1990	Trade 1980	1990	Business 1980	1990	Service 1980	1990	Public administration 1980	1990
White														
Unemployed	10.76	8.84	6.11	4.37	3.52	4.12	6.96	5.31	1.64	3.33	3.19	3.22	3.90	2.24
Working P-T	13.71	12.80	7.23	6.40	8.26	10.14	18.92	19.86	11.90	11.40	21.21	22.29	8.19	6.55
Working poor	8.13	7.33	5.92	6.13	4.37	4.12	10.28	11.05	5.51	4.75	9.69	8.57	5.65	3.62
Job mismatch	5.83	4.89	6.15	5.72	7.41	8.03	5.57	9.61	10.42	7.84	6.50	6.70	12.48	12.07
Asian Indian														
Unemployed	12.25	8.06	6.14	4.73	4.81	4.85	6.66	4.35	3.40	4.07	3.44	3.03	4.08	2.69
Working P-T	3.42	7.42	3.89	3.68	8.25	4.62	13.52	12.36	8.11	9.50	9.72	12.60	5.31	3.46
Working poor	6.55	5.81	9.42	7.23	5.84	6.24	12.72	14.11	12.64	4.26	6.41	6.91	2.45	3.08
Job mismatch	33.05	20.32	37.92	27.94	32.30	32.56	22.56	28.15	33.02	30.04	20.61	20.54	45.71	33.46
Filipino														
Unemployed	10.53	8.75	4.61	4.63	3.58	2.07	5.79	5.04	2.63	2.31	2.16	2.79	3.10	3.33
Working P-T	12.27	10.24	6.95	4.59	6.17	5.13	19.01	16.99	9.45	7.80	11.59	11.98	7.35	4.58
Working poor	8.56	8.01	10.73	6.91	4.20	4.69	11.29	11.46	8.63	4.93	8.54	7.47	6.58	4.58
Job mismatch	11.46	8.90	23.78	17.99	26.30	22.38	17.03	18.10	29.75	23.39	19.28	15.81	20.00	19.31
Vietnamese														
Unemployed	11.11	8.00	6.02	5.32	1.14	3.30	5.90	6.58	3.05	2.60	6.99	4.19	7.50	2.00
Working P-T	8.73	22.67	5.52	5.05	4.55	4.95	15.74	18.34	6.87	10.42	16.07	16.16	8.75	7.00
Working poor	10.32	8.00	14.24	7.41	12.50	5.49	17.21	14.89	11.45	8.33	13.10	9.54	17.50	3.00
Job mismatch	7.14	5.33	9.14	6.64	9.09	9.34	5.90	8.20	14.50	11.46	9.23	7.79	15.00	8.00

[a]Residual percentage for each cell reflects the distribution of the adequately employed.

administration sector. The diminished role of agriculture in the U.S. economy explains the magnitude of unemployment in this sector. The service industry is predominantly female which may explain the prevalence of part-time employment in this sector. A worsening economy coupled with failure of small businesses may explain the poverty of workers in trade, while high job mismatch in public administration may be attributed to the fact that employment integration among highly qualified immigrants is most prevalent in the public sector. In summary, bivariate analysis shows that underemployment occurs most in situations of low educational attainment, recent migrant status, younger age, female-headed households, and in agriculture and trade. These variables, as well as other control variables are used as determinants of labor force participation and underemployment, in the multivariate models discussed in the next two chapters.

Descriptive Profile of Asian Underemployment in the United States: A Summary

In this chapter I have documented the basic patterns of underemployment in general, by gender, and by selected independent variables, for 1980 and 1990. We find that total underemployment in both years is highest among Indians and lowest among the whites. Total underemployment of women is higher than that of men across ethnic groups and time frames. The largest gender differential in total underemployment was observed for whites in both years. The smallest gender differential was found among Filipinos in 1980 and the Indians in 1990. Unemployment was high for Vietnamese women and men in 1980 and 1990. Women's part-time work is highest in both years among whites and lowest among Filipinos. Among men, part-time work is highest among the Vietnamese and lowest among Indians. Working poverty among women is highest among the Vietnamese in 1980 and lowest among the Filipinos. By 1990, the highest rate of female working poverty is found among whites, with the Filipinos remaining as the group with the lowest female working poverty rate. Similarly for men, the Vietnamese have the highest working poverty rate in 1980 and 1990. For both years, male working poverty is lowest among the Indians. Job mismatch for both years is highest among Filipino women and lowest among white women. Men's job mismatch figures show Indians with the highest percentage of job mismatch and Vietnamese men with the lowest rate. The expected relationships between the selected independent variables and the types of underemployment are upheld in this bivariate analysis. Low and very high educational attainment, recent migrant status, younger age, female-headed households, and employment in agriculture and trade all contribute to higher incidences of underemployment. These descriptive results need to be tested in a multivariate setting. These will be pursued in the next two chapters. The majority of each group studied is adequately employed. The following discussion considers only the remaining four underemployment categories.

5

Determinants of Asian
Labor Force Participation

The selective nature of the study of underemployment necessitates an examination of labor force participation. Since the concept of underemployment requires that a person is employed or is actively looking for work, the nature of an underemployment study therefore focuses on a select group—those in the labor force. This becomes more critical in comparative studies of ethnic groups since selectivity issues become more pronounced because of the documented differences in their rates of labor force participation. Consequently, in this chapter, the issue of sample selectivity in underemployment is addressed by investigating determinants of labor force participation and by estimating a sample selection correction factor which will then be incorporated in the multivariate underemployment models in Chapter 6.

The labor force participation literature points to three major groups of factors that determine participation in the labor force: nativity and migrant status (Chiswick 1986; Sjastaad 1962), human capital (Becker 1965), and family considerations (Becker 1981; Blau and Ferber 1992). Unless migrating for the specific purpose of accepting a job offer, migrants are disadvantaged in their destination job market, primarily because of the absence of location-specific capital (DaVanzo 1981). Lack of knowledge about the new job market, absence of employment networks, and deficient information sources about jobs put migrants in a disadvantaged labor force participation position compared to natives in the destination area. Data on Asian Americans confirm this finding and show that native-born Asian American women are more likely to be in the labor force than the foreign-born (except for Indian and Filipino women) (Gardner, Robey, and Smith 1989).

Human capital factors also determine labor force participation. Jobs require a certain degree of skill and education, and those who do not have one or the other will have a difficult time finding a job. Particularly in a job market where education and credentialling is the norm (Kanter 1990), people without such credentials, skills, and experience are disadvantaged in getting a job. Since education increases productivity, and consequently earnings, people with higher education experience a high opportunity cost by staying away from the labor force. Therefore, labor force participation is expected to increase with higher levels of education. Blau and Ferber (1992) show that women's labor force participation rates increase from 45 percent for those with fewer than four years of high school in 1988 to 81 percent for those with four or more years of college.

The influence of family roles and responsibilities is primarily gender-based, affecting mostly women. The concept of opportunity cost argues that a person faced with the need to decide between two positions will choose the one that offers the most utility. In the choice, the person has to forgo whatever opportunities the other position offers. Becker's (1981) application of the concept of opportunity cost to a woman's work-versus-family dilemma is widely known. Women who have children have to decide whether to choose participation in the labor force or child rearing. Those who choose labor force participation often delay childbearing or look for alternative sources of childcare, like daycare centers or care by relatives. Those who decide to concentrate on child rearing stay out of the labor force. The family situation in the 1990s finds more and more men facing these same family concerns that were the monopoly of women in the past. In an effort to accommodate the modern family, employers have now introduced time-off of work for men who have a newborn or whose children are sick. The presence of small children deters the labor force participation of women (Blau and Ferber 1992). Gardner and colleagues (1989) show, however, that the labor force participation of Asian American women is still high, even when they have children under 18 living at home.

Another family factor in labor force participation is the concept of tied migration (Sandell 1977). Tied migration occurs when one partner moves to take a job in another area, and the other partner is forced to move, without necessarily having any job opportunities immediately available. The tied migrant therefore drops out of the labor force, usually temporarily, until readjustment to the new place has been completed. Previously a concern among married women, this has become a concern for both genders given the highly migratory nature of employment in the U.S. labor market. Through spousal employment referral services, contemporary employers have also attempted to address this problem of dual-career couples. Women who are married and whose spouse is present are generally less likely to work outside the home compared to other marital status categories (Blau and Ferber 1992). Married men, on the other hand, are more likely to be in the labor force than men in other marital status categories (Blau and Feber 1992). Findings from Gardner and associates (1989) support this situation, showing Asian American wives of male household heads have lower rates of labor force participation than female family household heads or women with no husband present.

Age is expected to have a positive effect on labor force participation. While labor force participation is assumed to be low at the younger ages because of enrollment in school, it is expected to increase with age, particularly after completion of formal schooling. Men, in particular, are presumed to remain in the labor force because of their traditional role responsibilities as the wage-earner of the family. Women, on the other hand, have been known to follow an inverted U-shaped labor force participation rate, with dips in the middle ages as they leave the labor force temporarily for childbearing and childrearing. An increase in the participation rates of younger women aged 20 to 44, particularly among married women with young children, has changed the labor force participation profile of women from the M-shaped one of the 1960s, to an inverted U-shaped one in the 1990s (Blau and Ferber 1992). The labor force participation profile of women now looks similar to that of men, with low participation rates at the younger ages, rising participation between the ages of 20 and 44, and then declining rates from then on until retirement. While the overall labor force participation rates of Asian Americans and non-Hispanic whites in 1990 were the same, young Asian Americans are less likely to be in the labor force while older Asians are more likely to remain in the labor force (O'Hare and Felt 1991).

These factors form the basis for the labor force participation model presented below. The negative transitory effect of migration is addressed through the migrant status variable measuring duration of stay in the United States (whether in the country for eleven years or more). Credentials and skills are proxied by the graduation from high school variable, defined as completion of twelve years or more of formal education. The negative effect of school attendance on labor force participation is controlled for by including a variable measuring whether the person is currently enrolled in school. Presence of children in the household and marital status are included to tap the family-related factors in labor force participation. Finally, age and age squared are included in the model to control for life-course trajectories that usually find rates of participation in the labor force highest in the early 20s (usually denoted by postcollege education), and waning as the individual gets older and moves toward retirement age.

Using the complete sample, the model found in Equation 3.1 is run for each of the four ethnic groups considered, gender, and each year under consideration. Results are discussed separately by gender in the succeeding sections of this chapter.

Labor Force Participation of Asian Women

Table 5.1 shows that most of the variables consistently determine the labor force participation of women across the ethnic groups considered in this study. The influence of migrant status on labor force participation is not significant for any of the women in 1980. However, migration status is a significant predictor of labor force participation in 1990 for all but Filipino women, showing older migrants and U.S.-born women as more likely to be in the labor force compared to more recent migrants. These findings support the migrant labor force disadvantage thesis discussed earlier. The changes between 1980 and 1990 are attributable to the increased labor force participation of women among the groups that until lately had lower labor force participation rates.

As expected, the correlation between formal education and labor force participation was highly significant and positive across all of the four ethnic groups considered. (Filipino women is the only exception to this trend, showing a significant negative relationship between education and labor force participation in 1990.) This finding reinforces the continued importance of formal education and credentialling in preparation for incorporation into the labor force. The expected negative relationship between school attendance and labor force participation is upheld for all the ethnic groups of women studied and for both years. Enrollment in school continues to keep women away from the labor force.

The presence of a young child in the household clearly affects the labor force participation of women in 1980 and 1990. Women who have young children in the household are consistently and significantly less likely to be in the labor force than women without young children in the household. Being married kept women out of the labor force in both years, with the effect for Vietnamese women losing significance in 1990. This general finding may reflect the traditional family roles of married couples, where men are the breadwinners in the family and women attend to household duties. The likelihood of labor force participation increases with age, so older women in the ethnic groups studied are

Table 5.1 Odds of female labor force participation by ethnic group and year

	Ethnic Group							
	Non-Hispanic white		Indian		Filipino		Vietnamese	
Independent variables	1980	1990	1980	1990	1980	1990	1980	1990
Years in U.S.	1.24	2.96***	1.00	1.33***	1.04	0.83***	1.35	1.98***
High school graduate+	.87***	3.20***	1.44***	1.76***	2.00***	0.42***	2.04***	2.69***
Attends school	0.37***	0.56***	0.62***	0.71***	0.57***	0.66***	0.46***	0.47***
Child <6 in HH	0.34***	0.36***	0.44***	0.45***	0.53***	0.54***	0.44***	0.42***
Married	0.44***	0.58***	0.54***	0.69***	0.56***	0.77***	0.81*	1.07
Age	1.13***	1.20***	1.30***	1.34***	1.34***	1.34***	1.22***	1.24***
Age squared	1.00	1.00	1.00***	1.00***	1.00***	1.00***	1.00***	1.00***
Intercept	0.38**	0.03***	0.03***	0.01***	0.02***	0.11***	0.06***	0.03***
-2 log likelihood	1136.62	1268.54	538.41	576.99	1649.47	1426.61	458.10	798.32
df	7	7	7	7	7	7	7	7
N	8804	9161	5759	5510	12031	12206	3628	4413

Significance levels: *** $p \leq 0.001$; ** $p \leq 0.01$; * $p \leq 0.05$.

more likely to be in the labor force in 1980 and 1990. This scenario reflects the increasing labor force participation among women, contrary to the expected M-shaped relationship between age and labor force participation. More and more women are now deciding to stay in the labor force despite family responsibilities (Blau and Ferber 1992).

In summary, labor force participation models for women provide support for most of the perspectives discussed above. Formal education (specifically high school graduation) and presence of a young child in the household and age were found to have the most consistent and significant effect on the labor force participation of all the women (regardless of ethnicity), across time. Migrant status also showed a consistent positive influence on labor force participation for most ethnic groups in 1990.

Labor Force Participation of Asian Men

The evidence shows weak and mixed effects of duration of stay in the United States on men's labor force participation (Table 5.2). The effect of duration of stay in the United States on the labor force participation of men was significant for whites and Filipinos. However, a longer stay in the United States means a greater likelihood of being in the labor force for white men, but a lesser likelihood of being in the labor force for Filipino men. The significance and directions of these findings continue in 1990, with the addition of a significant positive effect for Vietnamese men as well. The restructuring of the U.S. economy is hypothesized to be responsible, in part, for this opposite-from-expected effect for Filipinos. As discussed in Chapter 2, early migrants from the Philippines were manual laborers. Not until the early 1970s were migrants from both countries openly admitted based on occupational qualifications. The restructuring of the U.S. economy has led to the shift away from agricultural and manual-type jobs, to service and high technology communication jobs (Bluestone and Harrison 1982; Noyelle 1987). Currently, direct hiring from the origin countries for skilled high technology jobs is common-place in the U.S. labor market. The negative influence of tenure in the U.S. on Filipino labor force participation, therefore, may be related to this industrial shift. Findings for the Vietnamese is in the expected direction of migrant disadvantage, possibly because they are more likely to occupy blue-collar positions that are not in any of the industries experiencing an employment slump in 1990. The positive effect of migrant status for whites reflects the advantage of the native-born in the labor force.

Table 5.2 Odds of male labor force participation by ethnic group and year

Independent variables	Non-Hispanic white		Indian		Filipino		Vietnamese	
	1980	1990	1980	1990	1980	1990	1980	1990
Years in U.S.	2.16**	1.81*	1.10	1.05	0.86*	0.84*	1.04	1.61***
High school grad.+	1.88***	2.36***	1.21	2.28***	1.67***	1.96***	2.14***	2.69***
Attends school	0.24***	0.37***	0.22***	0.26***	0.30***	0.36***	0.34***	0.28***
Child <6 in HH	1.35*	nda	1.03	nda	0.94	nda	0.83*	nda
Married	2.52***	2.59***	1.80***	1.43**	1.84***	1.72***	1.42**	1.14
Age	1.21***	1.28***	1.45***	1.42***	1.40***	1.33***	1.23***	1.33***
Age squared	1.00***	1.00***	1.00***	1.00***	1.00***	1.00***	1.00***	1.00***
Intercept	0.11***	0.04***	0.01***	0.01***	0.02***	0.03***	0.06***	0.17***
-2 log likelihood	1512.89	1573.82	1460.30	1557.29	012.03	1807.37	690.71	1274.88
df	7	6	7	6	7	6	7	6
N	8704	9120	6561	6733	9554	9462	3790	4981

Note: nda = no data available

Significance levels: *** p<=0.001; ** p<=0.01; * p<=0.05.

High school graduation or higher educational backgrounds translate into a greater likelihood of labor force participation for whites, Filipinos, and Vietnamese in 1980. This significant effect remains for all ethnic groups in 1990. Consistent with human capital theory, people who are investing in education usually find themselves cashing in on their investments through participation in the labor force. This theory is supported by findings showing strong significant effects of school attendance on labor force participation for all ethnic groups and both years which means that similar to the situation for women, enrollment in school is a significant predictor of delayed entry into the labor force.

Unlike the results for women, the presence of children in the household has a positive effect on the labor force participation of white men, a nonsignificant effect for Filipino and Indian men, but a negative effect on the labor force participation of Vietnamese men in 1980. (The absence of data in 1990 makes time comparisons impossible.) The finding for whites is compatible with the traditional norm of men as breadwinners in the family, and is therefore consistent with expectations. Vietnamese men retreating from the labor force to care for a young child is unlikely based on the greater traditionalism expected among this ethnic group. However, it may be necessitated by the employment conditions faced by Vietnamese couples. As expected, married men are more likely to be in the labor force than unmarried men across all ethnic groups and years. This again is consistent with the traditional role of men as family breadwinners, necessitating their presence in the labor force.

The influence of age on the labor force participation of men shows a consistent and significant positive relationship for all ethnic groups and both years. This situation supports the typical life-course trajectory of men where they join the labor force after completing their education and stay until retirement. The lower labor force participation rate for younger men may reflect those who are enrolled in school full-time and have therefore not yet entered the labor force formally.

In summary, high school graduation is a positive and significant influence on male labor force participation across ethnic groups and time. School attendance kept men away from the labor force. Married men are consistently more likely to be in the labor force, for all ethnic groups and years considered. The influence of age is the same through time—positive and significant for white, Indian, Filipino, and Vietnamese men. Finally for 1980 only, white men with children in the household are more likely to be in the labor force.

Asian Labor Force Participation
and Sample Selection

The results presented above are incorporated into Equation 3.1 and the logit λ_t imputed for each ethnic group-gender-year combination. The symbol λ_i represents the sample selection correction factor. This correction factor is then included as a control variable in the multinomial models of underemployment discussed in the next chapter.

6

Determinants
of Asian Underemployment

Underemployment outcomes are theoretically linked to five groups of independent and control variables discussed in Chapter 1. In this chapter, the results of multinomial logistic regression analyses are presented, assessing the impact of the variables above on the different underemployment outcomes. Parameter estimates are computed as unstandardized beta coefficients and significance is assessed at the 99.99 percent confidence interval (p< = 0.001), 99 percent confidence interval (p< = 0.01), and 95 percent confidence interval (p< = 0.05). The parameter estimates are transformed from logodds to odds. They are presented and interpreted as the effect of X (independent variable) on the odds of the underemployment category (unemployed, employed part-time, working poverty, and job mismatch) against being adequately employed. A significant result that is greater than 1.0 means a positive relationship while a number less than 1.0 signifies a negative relationship. Results are presented separately by gender, ethnic group, and year.

Determinants of Underemployment
of Asian Women

Determinants of Unemployment

Support for the influence of human capital and family and household variables on unemployment is evident from the results. Some industry, demographic, and migration variable influences are also apparent, but not consistently across the ethnic groups (see Table 6.1).

The hypotheses discussed earlier predict the negative relationship of education to unemployment. The results of this relationship in 1980 showed education being positively related to unemployment across all ethnic groups, except for Filipino college graduates. In 1990, the signs changed for whites and Vietnamese, thereby supporting the aforementioned hypothesis, but remained the same for Indians and Filipinos.

Table 6.1 Odds of female unemployment by ethnic group[a] (reference category in parentheses)

Variables	White		Asian Indian		Filipino		Vietnamese	
	1980	1990	1980	1990	1980	1990	1980	1990
Human Capital								
HS grad+some coll (<HS)	2.77***	0.37**	1.32	1.00	2.72***	1.16	5.05**	0.84
Coll grad+postcoll (<HS)	2.01	0.18***	2.80	2.25*	0.33***	1.84*	11.25***	0.22*
Disability	1.02	2.41**	5.42*	2.14	1.35	4.39***	1.13	4.06*
Self-employed	0.90	0.52	0.72	0.41	2.01**	0.87	0.45	0.90
Family & Household								
Householder	0.07***	0.58**	0.14***	0.66	1.07	0.60***	0.14***	0.51**
No. workers in HH	0.02***	0.89*	0.02***	0.70***	1.04	0.91	0.05***	0.69***
Child <6 in HH	0.25***	1.75	0.77	1.15	1.02	0.77	0.76	1.25
Industry (Manufacturing)								
Agric/mining/const	1.00	1.009	1.80	1.60	1.27	0.39*	1.30	0.68
Transp & communications	0.65	0.51	0.19*	0.34*	0.90	0.28***	ni	0.93
Trade	1.66*	1.19	0.52*	0.53*	1.05	0.14***	0.66	0.90
Business	0.22**	0.35***	0.18***	0.21***	1.06	0.13***	0.32	0.46
Service	0.55*	0.60*	0.11***	0.19***	2.72***	0.18***	0.73	0.42**
Public administration	0.56	0.27*	0.16*	0.33*	1.30	0.25***	0.71	0.38

Demographics								
31–45 yrs (16–30 yrs)	0.63*	0.66*	1.16	1.35	0.88	1.06	0.87	1.21
46–64 yrs (16–30 yrs)	0.03***	0.40***	0.19***	2.14**	0.73**	1.18	0.36	1.11
Migration & Language								
Migrated < = 10 yrs (Nat)	3.35	1.36	4.85***	4.95*	0.38***	1.88**	1.51	0.39
Migrated 11+ yrs (Nat)	1.92	0.47	4.26***	2.46	0.56***	1.19	3.82	0.30
Fluent in English	0.92	0.97	0.72	0.83	0.23***	0.94	0.84	0.54**
Sample Selection Factor	0.12***	0.88	0.23***	0.68	0.90	0.46***	0.16**	0.76
Intercept	1188.0***	0.96	343.8	0.29	24.05***	1.05	33.12*	3.78
Likelihood Ratio X^2	5566.6	6979.6	4510.2	4656.6	11382.2	11404.8	410.2	3577.9
Degrees of Freedom	9193	11300	7252	7340	17760	19468	762	6433

[a]Models estimated using simultaneous multinomial logistic regression; models with missing variables (ni) with binary logistic regression.

What happened in 1980 that supported a positive relationship between education and unemployment? Why do the Indian and Filipino
women consistently hold that positive relationship in spite of changes in
the experiences of whites and Vietnamese? Women with higher education are expected to have better chances of gaining employment in the
labor market than those with lower educational attainment. However,
this hypothesis is not supported by the results of Indian and Filipino
women; in fact, the results for these two groups were significant, but in
the opposite direction. This unexpected result can be partly attributed to
the general characteristic of migrants from these countries. Table 6.1
shows that the positive effect of education on unemployment occurs
when the effect of migrant status also is significant. Therefore, the influence of education is mediated by the migrant status of these women.
Indian and Filipino migrants in general, particularly the more recent
migrants, arrive in the United States with high educational attainments,
but because of the circumstances that accompany migrant status, they
are less likely to translate these educational attainments into employment when compared to whites.

Having a limiting disability is an important characteristic that kept
the women (except the Indian women where the effect of disability was
significant in 1980) from being employed in 1990. The results for disability are consistent with expectations specified earlier.

Being a household head and the number of workers in the household appeared as consistent predictors of unemployment across years
and ethnic groups. As expected, household heads are less likely to be
unemployed than those who are not household heads. However, the expected positive relationship of number of workers in the household, which
is supposed to measure earnings potential for the household, did not
hold. It was hypothesized that having more alternative sources of income (more workers in the household) provides women with the option
of being unemployed or out of the labor force, especially if there is a
young child in the household. The results show a negative relationship
instead, across all ethnic groups. Unemployed women therefore come
from households with fewer workers. Having a young child in the household did not have any significant effect on unemployment of women,
except for the negative effect for whites in 1980.

Unemployment of women appears to be most prevalent in the
manufacturing sector compared to any other industry as evidenced by
the significant negative relationship of almost all the other industries
when compared to manufacturing. In particular, the service sector was

the one most consistent in showing a lesser likelihood of being unemployed compared to the manufacturing sector, across ethnic groups. That these effects are strongest reflects deindustrialization in the U.S. economy, best characterized by the decline of the manufacturing sector (Bluestone and Harrison 1982).

The influence of age on unemployment shows mixed and inconsistent results. White women reflect the results most consistent with the hypothesis that younger women are more likely to be unemployed. Results show that the influence of age on unemployment for whites is consistently negative and significant, for Indian women is inconsistent for the older group compared to the younger reference group, for Filipinos is mixed in 1980, and is not present for Vietnamese women. Younger white women appear to be the age group suffering most from unemployment (Table 6.1). Being in the older group served to decrease the likelihood of being unemployed in 1980 among Indians, but even this changed to a positive relationship in 1990. Among Filipinos in 1980, older women are less likely to experience unemployment than their younger counterparts.

The effect of migrant status on unemployment is evident from the experiences of Indian and Filipino women. Consistent with expectations, Indian migrants were more likely to be unemployed than their native-born counterparts in 1980 and 1990. For Filipino women, however, migrants are less likely than the native-born to be unemployed in 1980, although this relationship turns positive in 1990. In addition to this, there is also support for the assimilation thesis, as shown by the decreasing importance of migrant status in 1990 with increased tenure in the United States. Surprisingly, there is no effect of migrant status on the unemployment of Vietnamese women, although English language proficiency appeared to be the more important determinant of unemployment. However, this result later on became feasible given the refugee status of Vietnamese women. Their refugee status overcomes the difficulties faced by other migrant groups of getting legal work permission. In fact, the Vietnamese may benefit from government-sponsored employment programs (Rutledge 1992) meant to facilitate their integration into American society. Language difficulties appeared to be a hindrance to gainful employment for the Vietnamese, a problem evident also among Filipino women in 1980.

Women's unemployment appears to be determined most consistently by household head status and the number of workers in the family, as well as some evidence of industry effects. Mixed effects are apparent for the human capital and age variables, for the different ethnic groups. Migration and language variables are important for the migrant groups, with duration of stay in the United States critical for Indian and Filipino women, and English language proficiency important for Filipino and Vietnamese women.

Determinants of Part-time Employment

The classical Labor Utilization Framework (LUF) categorization considered only involuntary part-time work as evidence of under-employment (Clogg 1979; Sullivan 1978). Because of data limitations, such an operationalization of part-time work is not possible in this study. As such, part-time work in this study covers voluntary and involuntary part-time work. This operationalization is not problematic for women, since the part-time employment models were able to control for the family factors believed to be mostly responsible for keeping the women from full-time employment and making them opt for voluntary part-time employment. The results of the female part-time employment models appear in Table 6.2.

The effects of education on part-time employment are limited to scattered influences on white, Indian, and Filipino women, where higher education usually translated to a greater likelihood of part-time employment. There is reason to believe that a composition effect is working here, and an extension of this argument from the unemployment model discussion is very likely. There are more white, Indian, and Filipino women who are highly educated in the labor force and therefore this composition effect can determine the employment outcomes of these women, part-time employment included.

It appears that disability and self-employment are the major human capital predictors of part-time employment, particularly for white and Filipino women in 1990. Self-employment seems to be an adaptive mechanism for women who by choice or circumstance cannot get a full-time job.

Consistent with expectations from the labor-market-restructuring and deindustrialization literature, part-time employment is most prevalent in the "emerging" industries of trade (except for Filipinos) and service and less so in the declining manufacturing industry. The inverted U-shaped trend typical in the age and labor force participation relationship can be extended to characterize the observed relationship between age and number of hours worked. Middle-aged women are more likely to be employed part-time compared to young women and older women are less likely to be employed part-time than young women. Surprisingly, the family and household variables attributed to the U-shaped age and labor force participation trend do not figure significantly in predicting part-time employment. Although bereft of explanation, a positive pattern towards part-time employment around middle age is apparent among whites, Indians, and Filipinos.

There is some evidence in support of the assimilation hypothesis. Indian, Filipino, and Vietnamese women who are fluent in the English language are less likely to be employed part-time. However, part-time employment appears to be characteristic of native-born Indians and Filipinos rather than of migrants. Part-time employment therefore does not appear to be an employment strategy for Indian and Filipino women given an option for full-time, adequate employment.

Determinants of Working Poor Status

The literature presented in the earlier chapters provides a statement on the typical setting for a working poor environment. Female household headship, single parenting, minority status, young age, and low wages characterize working poverty for women (Gardner and Herz 1992). The results of this study reveal determinants of working poor status that are consistent with the literature. Table 6.3 shows that self-employment, family headship, industry, and English language capability are among the more reliable determinants of female working poor status.

Across ethnic groups, it appears that the most consistent determinants of working poor status are self-employment and industry. Education did not play a significant role in determining working poor status except for white and Filipino women in 1990, and it had a slightly significant effect for Indian women in 1980. There is some semblance of a limiting disability effect on working poor status, although such effects are not generalizable across time or ethnic group. The significant effects of having a work-limiting disability on working poor status are more apparent in 1980 than 1990, among whites, Indians, and Filipinos. The single most important human capital variable that affects working poor status is self-employment, where the women are most likely to be working but in poverty, if they are self-employed. This trend is most apparent in 1990 than in 1980, but some evidence of a significant effect of this variable in 1980 is present for whites and Filipinos. Self-employment appears to be a coping strategy among women who cannot otherwise find jobs, or prefer not to be employed full-time. A usual explanation

Table 6.2 Odds of part-time female employment by ethnic group[a] (reference category in parentheses)

Variables	White		Indian		Filipino		Vietnamese	
	1980	1990	1980	1990	1980	1990	1980	1990
Human Capital								
HS grad+some coll (<HS)	1.23	1.95***	0.90	0.84	4.57***	1.34	0.94	1.25
Coll grad+postcoll (<HS)	1.27	1.86**	1.43*	1.84*	0.48**	1.75***	1.09	1.09
Disability	2.46***	2.05***	1.79	0.91	1.779	3.32***	0.78	3.74**
Self-employed	1.58**	2.22***	1.62*	1.45*	1.97	2.48***	1.19	1.45
Family & Household								
Householder	0.07***	0.88	1.51	1.28	0.18***	0.98	1.02	0.65*
No. workers in HH	0.02***	1.08**	1.39**	1.06	0.04***	1.11**	0.75*	0.93
Child <6 in HH	0.92	1.17	1.21	1.17	1.31	0.997	1.04	0.98
Industry (Manufacturing)								
Agric/mining/const	4.14***	2.08**	1.68	1.63	1.61	2.14*	1.70	3.94**
Transp & communications	1.32	1.93***	2.27*	1.84	0.28**	3.39***	2.80	0.64
Trade	4.26***	4.18***	4.48***	4.95***	0.78	1.02	3.06***	4.53***
Business	1.68**	1.09	1.54	1.92*	0.37***	1.54*	1.02	1.77
Service	3.29***	3.06***	1.55*	2.08***	0.52**	0.61	4.00***	3.94***
Public administration	1.23	0.73	1.03	1.17	0.66	0.70	1.42	1.20

Demographics								
31–45 yrs (16–30 yrs)	1.43***	1.30**	1.09	1.70**	1.38	1.46**	0.89	1.13
46–64 yrs (16–30 yrs)	0.69	0.71**	0.94	1.17	0.35***	1.06	0.83	1.05
Migration & Language								
Migrated < = 10 yrs (nat)	1.57	0.38	0.52***	0.73	0.59*	0.80	0.64	0.74
Migrated 11+ yrs (nat)	1.80**	1.21	0.85	0.70	0.54*	0.77*	0.76	0.90
Fluent in English	1.70	0.93	0.55*	0.88	0.30**	0.91	0.77	0.67*
Sample Selection Factor	0.44***	0.43***	0.69*	0.70	0.26***	0.54***	0.82	0.62
Intercept	0.12***	0.21**	0.17***	0.13***	2892.7***	0.21***	0.43	0.29
Likelihood Ratio X^2	5566.6	6079.6	4520.3	4656.6	11392.2	22404.8	2479.6	3577.9
Degrees of Freedom	9193	11300	7525	7340	17760	19468	4422	6433

[a] Models estimated using simultaneous multinomial logistic regression; models with missing variables (ni) with binary logistic regression.

Table 6.3 Odds of female working poor status by ethnic group[a] (reference category in parentheses)

Variables	White		Indian		Filipino		Vietnamese	
	1980	1990	1980	1990	1980	1990	1980	1990
Human Capital								
HS grad+some coll (<HS)	0.77	0.64	0.66*	0.79	2.22***	1.27	0.90	1.16
Coll grad+postcoll (<HS)	0.67	0.35***	1.34	1.22	0.30***	1.23	0.95	1.02
Disability	2.10**	1.34	3.82**	1.14	2.94*	1.95*	0.61	2.59
Self-employed	2.32***	3.82***	1.22	2.03**	3.29***	2.14***	1.60	1.88*
Family & Household								
Householder	0.38***	0.52***	0.53**	0.84	1.35*	0.62***	1.12	0.57
No. workers in HH	0.98	1.15**	1.05	1.20*	1.12	1.05	1.03	0.96
Child <6 in HH	1.05	1.17	0.54	0.95	1.11	0.68**	1.05	0.76
Industry (Manufacturing)								
Agric/ining/const	2.83***	1.06	1.84	1.08	2.41**	2.36*	0.73	ni
Transp & communications	0.76	0.84	0.90	0.46	0.68	2.22**	0.70	1.11
Trade	2.01***	2.18***	1.40	2.72***	3.94***	0.76	1.42	2.48***
Business	0.76	0.68	1.38	0.70	1.30	1.07	0.98	0.76
Service	1.65**	1.60**	0.53***	1.07	3.63***	0.92	1.36	1.52*
Public administration	0.99	0.73	0.38	0.84	1.46	1.09	2.94*	0.91

	Model 1	Model 2	Model 3	Model 4	Model 5	Model 6	Model 7	Model 8
Demographics								
31–45 yrs (16–30 yrs)	0.81	0.71**	0.82	1.12	1.20	1.25	0.80	0.92
46–64 yrs (16–30 yrs)	0.44***	0.44***	0.53*	0.67	0.55***	0.72*	0.68	0.70
Migration & Language								
Migrated <= 10 yrs (nat)	0.32	1.00	1.90**	1.97	0.59*	2.34***	2.18	0.71
Migrated 11+ yrs (nat)	0.74	0.58	1.25	0.98	0.49***	1.02	1.45	0.46
Fluent in English	ni	2.77	0.61*	0.47***	0.25***	0.89	0.62**	0.72
Sample Selection Factor	0.71*	0.65**	0.53**	0.63	0.62***	0.48***	0.93	0.76
Intercept	0.64	0.20	0.91	0.21*	6.30***	0.28***	0.16	0.58
Likelihood Ratio X^2	1555.7	6979.6	4510.2	4656.6	11382.2	11404.8	2479.6	985.9
Degrees of Freedom	1598	11300	7252	7340	17760	19468	4422	1157

[a] Models estimated using simultaneous multinomial logistic regression; models with missing variables (ni) with binary logistic regression.

for self-employment would be the conflicting requirements of childrearing and employment on the women (Becker 1980), but the absence of any significant positive influence of the presence of a young child in the household does not allow such a conclusion. The inclination is to conclude that these women who are among the working poor are those who want to be employed, or otherwise could not land full-time jobs.

Fortunately, women household heads are not as likely to be working in poverty as some of the literature would suggest. More so, Indian and Filipino women who have a young child in the household are also less likely to be among the working poor. Contrary to previous findings, family considerations or situations do not seem to contribute to the incidence of working poverty among women.

Employment in the trade sector translates to a greater probability of working poverty for all groups of women, and more so in 1990 than in 1980. At the same time, employment in the service sector increases the likelihood of working in poverty among white and Vietnamese women, but decreases it for Indian women. This may be attributed to the types of jobs that the different groups of women take within the service sector, with Indian and Filipino women taking on the higher level ones and whites and Vietnamese the lower level ones. The kind of jobs in the trade sector that translate into working poverty status are mostly in retail sales jobs and the like. Some positive significant effects of employment in the agriculture/mining/construction sector for whites and particularly for Filipinos are observed, as well as the public administration sector for Vietnamese.

Although some age effects are present, mostly with older cohorts being less likely than the youngest one to be working in poverty, the strongest age effects are among whites, and among the oldest white, Indian, and Filipino women in 1980. Assimilation effects are strong among the recent Indian migrants in 1980 and Filipino recent migrants in 1990, who were more likely to be working in poverty than their native-born counterparts. In support of the literature (Borjas 1986; Chiswick 1986), the results for Indian and Filipino women show that recent migrants are indeed disadvantaged in the labor force on arrival at the destination, and one of their economic integration strategies is to accept marginal jobs or jobs that do not pay well. Since there is no accompanying significant education effect, it appears that this initial migrant disadvantage is common across all educational categories (except probably those who migrated to this country specifically to fill a job, such as nurses). Curiously, Filipino migrants in 1980 are less likely than their native-born counterparts to be in poverty while holding a full-time job. Nonproficiency in the English language also contributes to working poverty status across all Asian ethnic groups in this study, as evidenced by the finding that women from these groups who are fluent in the English language are less likely to be among the working poor.

In short, women who are working and in poverty are usually self-employed, not a household head, in the trade industry, younger, a recent migrant, and not proficient in the English language.

Determinants of Job Mismatch

Significant effects of advanced education, self-employment, and migration are apparent in the job mismatch models. As mentioned earlier, this is viewed as the most relevant model of Asian economic assimilation, given the high human capital attributes of Asians in the United States. The results shown in Table 6.4 reflect some truth to the statement above, but not for all of the immigrant groups considered.

Looking across Table 6.4, there seem to be fixed strong and consistent determinants of job mismatch among and across the different ethnic groups. In regard to human capital, two general trends are evident: the strong positive and significant effect of advanced education on mismatch. Job mismatch appears to be the exclusive experience of the highly educated—those who at least finished college. Mismatch is most likely among college graduates across ethnic groups, in 1980 and 1990 (with the exception of Filipinos in 1980). High school graduates and those with some college education were less likely than those with less than a high school education to be mismatched in 1980, although this changed to a positive relationship in 1990 for Filipinos and Vietnamese. In fact, three of the ethnic groups show that in 1980, the next educational group (those who at least finished high school) was even less likely to experience mismatch than those who had less than a high school education. It becomes interesting when Filipino and Vietnamese results showed a positive influence of high school graduation (or more) on mismatch, indicating the expansion of the mismatch experience to include high school graduates. A likely explanation for mismatch in general is the labor market situation of available jobs and the migrant disadvantage on economic assimilation. However, the expansion of the mismatch experience to include Filipino and Vietnamese high school graduates may be indicative of the characteristics of the more recent immigrant flow from these countries.

Table 6.4 Odds of female job mismatch by ethnic group[a] (reference category in parentheses)

Variables	White		Indian		Filipino		Vietnamese	
	1980	*1990*	*1980*	*1990*	*1980*	*1990*	*1980*	*1990*
Human Capital								
HS grad+some coll (<HS)	0.28***	1.40	0.22***	0.44	2.64***	5.20**	2.27	11.13*
Coll grad+postcoll (<HS)	6.62***	41.26***	2.74***	24.78***	0.35***	179.47***	120.30***	212.72***
Disability	1.46	0.33	0.36	0.90	2.16	0.57	ni	1.58
Self-employed	2.18*	1.15	0.29***	1.13	3.19***	0.81	3.46	2.22*
Family & Household								
Householder	0.52*	0.74	0.73	0.79	0.58***	0.92	1.17	0.68
No. workers in HH	0.76	0.97	1.15	1.16*	0.99	1.07*	1.43	0.96
Child <6 in HH	1.31	1.33	1.46	1.97*	0.78	0.90	1.13	0.63
Industry (Manufacturing)								
Agric/mining/const	1.75	0.44	1.63	0.61	1.51	0.36**	0.20	0.68
Transp & communications	1.26	1.04	1.06	2.14*	0.24***	1.49*	0.19	0.94
Trade	0.93	3.97***	0.88	1.45	1.12	0.67*	0.56	3.35***
Business	1.58	1.40	0.81	0.92	0.72	0.36***	0.42	1.30
Service	0.58*	0.74	0.30***	0.41***	1.68***	0.54***	0.32**	1.23
Public administration	1.14	1.51	1.09	0.96	1.12	0.87	1.11	0.40

Demographics								
31–45 yrs (16–30 yrs)	1.12	0.95	0.79	1.72**	0.74*	1.42***	0.69	1.86*
46–64 yrs (16–30 yrs)	0.79	1.25	0.73	2.46***	0.44***	1.90***	0.95	2.20
Migration & Language								
Migrated < = 10 yrs (nat)	2.12	8.76***	1.77*	3.74**	0.59**	1.82***	3.03	1.19
Migrated 11+ yrs (nat)	1.55	1.15	2.29**	2.05	0.42***	0.99	1.65	0.85
Fluent in English	0.95	0.85	1.19	0.87	0.30**	0.95	0.84	1.52
Sample Selection Factor	1.12	1.28	1.66*	1.86	0.54***	0.92	1.62	0.90
Intercept	0.19	0.01	0.22**	0.01***	16.44***	0.01***	0.004***	0.002***
Likelihood Ratio X^2	5566.6	6979.62	4510.2	4656.6	11382.2	11404.8	287.7	3577.9
Degrees of Freedom	9193	11300	7252	7340	17760	19468	704	6433

[a] Models estimated using simultaneous multinomial logistic regression; models with missing variables (ni) with binary logistic regression.

Two contradictory trends for self-employment are observed: negative for Indians and positive for whites, Filipinos, and Vietnamese. The contradictory influence of self-employment on mismatch for whites, Filipinos, and Vietnamese on one hand and Indians on the other may be because the type of self-employment of the former is in the form of businesses or enterprises (suitable to varied educational backgrounds), while Indians open professional practices (medicine, law, etc.).

Industry of employment shows two particularly consistent patterns across groups and time: (1) mismatch is less likely with employment in the service sector in 1980 (and 1990 for Indians and Filipinos) and (2) trade-sector employment increases the probability of mismatch in 1990 for whites and Vietnamese but not for Filipinos. A weak positive effect of employment in transportation and communication is observed for Indian and Filipino women in 1990. Employment in the service sector does not translate to mismatch possibly because most service workers are either lower level (clerks, aides, etc.) or managerial. As shown from the education results above, mismatch is less likely among workers with less education and therefore service workers with low levels of education will not be mismatched. At the other extreme, managers in the service industry are more likely than not to possess the qualifications of the position (since upward mismatch is not estimated, the incidence of such for service-sector managers cannot be ignored) and again they do not reflect mismatch. At the same time, the service industry is believed to have taken over the manufacturing jobs in most of the United States, implying that natives are occupying these positions more than migrants are. This is supported by the weaker influence of service-sector employment on mismatch for whites compared to the three Asian groups considered. Employment in trade increases the possibility of mismatch for possibly two reasons. First, this sector has historically been one in which immigrant economic incorporation has been successful as evidenced by the establishment of enterprise enclaves among Chinese, Indians, and Koreans, to name a few. It follows that recent migrants are most likely to gain their initial employment via networks, and these immigrant enterprises will be their first stop. Second, the trade sector is one of the growing industries in the United States (together with the service sector) at present, and its significant relationship to mismatch may just be indicative of its having more jobs available than the manufacturing sector.

Curiously, no age effects are evident in predicting mismatch among white women, but age effects are important for predicting mismatch of the migrant groups. In general, mismatch is more prevalent among the older age groups compared to the younger (16–30) age groups. Age is negatively associated with mismatch among Filipinos in 1980. This relationship changes in 1990, with Indians and Vietnamese added to the groups showing a significant positive relationship. The increased incidence of mismatch among the older age groups can be indicative of the reorganization of the workplace, characterized by the need for re-education to accommodate the information technology predominant in the workplace.

Most interesting are the migration and language results, which reflect strong evidence in support of the migrant disadvantage hypothesis. Results show that recent migrants are more apt than natives to be mismatched, an experience shared by white, Indian, and Filipino migrants.

The results of modeling underemployment for women reveal different variables as significant in determining the different categories of underemployment. Among human capital variables, education is most important in the mismatch and unemployment models. Disability is significant in the unemployment and part-time models, while self-employment is important in the part-time and working poor models. Family and household variables are most important in the unemployment and the working poor models. The effects of industry are varied, but significant in almost all the models, with the service and trade industries having the most effect across models. Age effects are important, but their influence is scattered across the different ethnic groups and models. Migration effects are most common among the Indians and Filipinos and span all of the underemployment models. The most significant migration results are among the recent migrants who are more likely to be unemployed, working poor, and mismatched, and less likely to be employed part-time.

Determinants of Underemployment of Asian Men

Determinants of Unemployment

The results for men's unemployment models appear in Table 6.5. Across ethnic groups, family and household variables as well as some human capital variables are the more significant predictors of unem-ployment in men.

Except for whites, education is not an important determinant of unemployment among men. With few and scattered effects across ethnic groups, education seems to help only white men from being unem-

Table 6.5 Odds of male unemployment by ethnic group^a (reference category in parentheses)

Variables	White 1980	White 1990	Indian 1980	Indian 1990	Filipino 1980	Filipino 1990	Vietnamese 1980	Vietnamese 1990
Human Capital								
HS grad+some coll (<HS)	0.79	0.51***	0.89	0.92	1.15	0.74	2.89*	1.34
Coll grad+postcoll (<HS)	0.69	0.35***	1.27	1.32	2.36***	1.16	2.89	1.58
Disability	1.77	3.52***	3.82^a	6.11***	4.90***	4.01***	3.00	6.05***
Self-employed	0.60	0.59*	0.46*	0.51*	0.54	1.35	2.34	0.83
Family & Household								
Householder	0.02***	0.31***	0.01***	0.26***	0.04***	0.43***	0.02***	0.40***
No. workers in HH	0.004***	0.96	0.01***	1.06	0.04***	1.04	0.01***	0.83**
Industry (Manufacturing)								
Agric/mining/const	3.22***	2.69***	1.04	0.89	2.66***	1.68*	0.89	1.53
Transp & communications	1.11	1.12	1.08	0.99	1.63	0.59	0.22	0.22*
Trade	1.72*	1.17	1.08	0.70	1.97**	1.20	0.62	0.96
Business	0.68	1.55	0.68	0.91	1.39	0.38*	0.23	0.26
Service	1.04	1.25	0.46**	0.50**	0.73	0.58**	0.91	0.68
Public administration	1.11	0.70	0.84	0.16*	0.62	0.74	0.45	0.21

Demographics								
31–45 yrs (16–30 yrs)	0.48***	1.01	1.04	1.65*	0.99	0.95	1.93	1.32
46–64 yrs (16–30 yrs)	0.19***	0.79	1.52	1.92**	0.73	0.75	1.65	0.86
Migration & Language								
Migrated < = 10 yrs (nat)	1.31	2.22	2.25	0.54	1.72**	1.14	1.58	0.90
Migrated 11+ yrs (nat)	1.70	0.84	1.19	0.36**	0.86	0.87	0.36	0.89
Fluent in English	1.18	0.52	0.58	0.42**	0.92	0.87	0.50*	0.65*
Sample Selection Factor	0.60**	0.81	0.92	0.71*	0.65**	0.53***	0.26**	0.47***
Intercept	788.40***	0.83	595.86***	1.66	46.06***	0.71	244.69***	1.26
Likelihood Ratio X^2	6700.0	7747.6	5414.28	6328.0	10296.1	8569.7	2788.5	4338.3
Degrees of Freedom	12724	14444	9916	11224	17392	16844	5409	8737

[a] Models estimated using simultaneous multinomial logistic regression; models with missing variables (m) with binary logistic regression.

ployed, and only in 1990. The most important human capital variable, which fosters unemployment across the ethnic groups considered is having a limiting disability. Its effects are more pervasive in 1990 than in 1980. These results point to two conclusions regarding human capital effects on unemployment. First is that education, particularly in 1990, is an insurance against unemployment only among white men. Men from the three Asian groups are equally likely to be unemployed regardless of education. Disability seems to be on the rise across all ethnic groups as it characterized more and more unemployed men. It is unclear whether there is an actual rise in the number of disabled men between 1980 and 1990 that causes this trend, or whether the gloomy labor market situation pushed men who turned out to be unemployed into admitting to a disability so that they could claim benefits, or whether the tight labor market resulted in employers firing disabled workers first.

As mentioned earlier, family and household variables are strong predictors of unemployment across all four ethnic groups. In each group, being a household head and having more workers in the household decreases the likelihood of being unemployed. In a household, the head is the primary breadwinner and it is heartening to note that they are not likely victims of unemployment. The unemployed also find themselves in households with fewer workers.

Only a few industry effects are significant and consistent across at least two ethnic groups. White and Filipino men employed in the agriculture/mining/construction industry are more likely to be unemployed than their counterparts in manufacturing for both years. At the same time, white and Filipino men employed in the trade sector in 1980 are also more likely than their counterparts in manufacturing to be unemployed. On the other hand, Indian and Filipino men employed in the service sector have decreased chances of being unemployed, compared to those in manufacturing. The instability of agriculture and construction work in particular is reflected in the increased likelihood of unemployment of men in these industries, at least among whites and Filipinos. The emerging service sector seems to be active in absorbing male Indian and Filipino labor.

Other than the significant negative relationship of age to unemployment of white men in 1980 and the significant positive relationship of age to unemployment of Indian men in 1990, unemployment is not characteristic of any particular age group of men. Men of different age groups are equally likely to be unemployed, a finding consistent across all ethnic groups in 1990.

Finally, support for the assimilation hypothesis is shown in the results, but only for Filipinos and Vietnamese men. Filipino recent migrants in 1980 are found to be more likely to be unemployed, compared to their native-born counterparts. Older Indian migrants in 1990 exhibit some form of assimilation by being less likely than the native-born to be unemployed. Consistent with the assimilation hypothesis and previous studies (Chiswick 1991; Kossoudji 1988; Sjastaad 1962), English language proficiency translated to better chances of employment for Indian and Vietnamese men in 1980 and 1990.

Determinants of Part-time Employment

Assessing the determinants of part-time employment is not as complicated as doing the same for women given that employment is a forgone assumption for men (and the same cannot be said for women). When modeling overall part-time employment as an underemployment category for men, it is safe to assume that what is being estimated is comparable to estimating the involuntary part-time work category in the traditional Labor Force Utilization Framework. As a result, controlling for having a young child in the household is disregarded, on the assumption that the work-childrearing dilemma affects only women. The results of modeling part-time employment appear in Table 6.6.

Human capital factors play an important role in determining part-time employment among the ethnic groups studied. Education does not figure significantly except negatively for whites and positively for Indians and Vietnamese, all in 1980. By 1990, there is no education effect on part-time employment. The negative relationship of education and part-time employment for whites is in line with the hypothesis of higher education's contributing to better (adequate) employment. Having a higher education paid off for whites in 1980. For Vietnamese men, having higher education translates to part-time employment which can be a positive situation given the difficulties that migrants have in assimilating into the labor market. Part-time employment can be seen as "at least getting a job." By 1990, however, the absence of an education effect means that men are equally likely to be working part-time, regardless of their education. This may be because of the tightening conditions in the labor market. Having a limiting disability increases the likelihood of being employed part-time across ethnic groups, and more so in 1990 than in 1980. Similarly, those who are self-employed are more likely to be working part-time than those who are not self-employed.

Table 6.6 Odds of part-time male employment by ethnic group[a] (reference category in parentheses)

Variables	White		Indian		Filipino		Vietnamese	
	1980	1990	1980	1990	1980	1990	1980	1990
Human Capital								
HS grad+some coll (<HS)	0.71*	1.02	1.01	1.54	1.25	0.93	2.59*	1.36
Coll grad+postcoll (<HS)	0.63*	1.09	1.90**	1.57	1.30	1.39	2.72*	1.05
Disability	2.92***	4.31***	2.32	3.42**	2.25**	2.03*	1.99	2.34*
Self-employed	1.82***	1.90***	0.89	1.97***	1.42	2.01***	2.27	1.14
Family & Household								
Householder	0.58***	0.58***	0.25***	0.54**	0.58**	0.65**	0.66	0.72
No. workers in HH	1.11	1.01	0.76	1.06	0.95	1.12*	0.93	0.91
Industry (Manufacturing)								
Agric/mining/const	2.18***	2.94***	0.85	2.22*	1.22	1.99**	2.18	8.50***
Transp & communications	1.32	1.55*	1.95	1.20	0.67	1.21	ni	1.52
Trade	1.18	2.34***	1.70	2.48***	1.11	3.56***	3.10***	5.10***
Business	0.90	1.73*	2.08*	1.65	1.05	1.58	1.43	4.57***
Service	1.79***	2.74***	1.13	2.86***	0.80	2.10***	3.35***	3.10***
Public administration	1.09	1.51	1.54	0.24	0.53*	1.15	3.29	2.43

Demographics								
31–45 yrs (16–30 yrs)	0.58***	0.84	1.38	1.40	1.28	1.00	2.18**	0.93
46–64 yrs (16–30 yrs)	0.41***	0.45***	1.48	0.87	0.71*	0.87	0.43*	0.92
Migration & Language								
Migrated <= 10 yrs (nat)	0.91	0.60	0.69	0.96	1.16	0.82	1.08	1.35
Migrated 11+ yrs (nat)	0.36*	0.92	0.53	0.73	1.14	0.73*	1.31	0.95
Fluent in English	0.79	0.55	0.81	0.59	0.90	0.65	0.58*	0.53***
Sample Selection Factor	0.69***	0.51	0.72	0.48***	0.60	0.54***	0.18***	0.70
Intercept	0.55	0.69	0.69	0.43	0.68	0.40**	0.39	0.17*
Likelihood Ratio X^2	6700.0	7747.6	5414.3	6328.0	10296.7	8569.1	610.6	4338.3
Degrees of Freedom	12724	14444	9916	11224	17392	16844	901	8737

[a] Models estimated using simultaneous multinomial logistic regression; models with missing variables (ni) with binary logistic regression.

While no family or household variable is significant for Vietnamese men, heading a household translated to a decreased likelihood of working part-time for the other male ethnic groups. This is consistent with the hypothesis that since household heads are the primary breadwinners of the family or household, they are more likely to seek adequate employment first before considering any other kind of (under)employment.

Some consistent industry results show that employment in the agriculture/mining /construction, trade, and service industries translates to a greater likelihood of working part-time across all ethnic groups when compared to their manufacturing industry counterparts. These industry effects are more prominent in 1990 than in 1980. At the same time, business industry employment also translates to increased probability of part-time employment, but only for three (whites, Indian, and Vietnamese) of the four groups. These industry effects are partly a function of changing labor economies, job characteristics, and industry characteristics. Manufacturing is labor intensive and stability is important, therefore full-time employment is characteristic of it. Agriculture/mining/construction is basically unstable, and like trade and service industries accommodates part-time employment without much loss of efficiency. Therefore, compared to manufacturing, these industries are more likely to have part-time employment because the structure of the industries and of the jobs in them can allow for part-time employment without affecting overall production or output.

Age effects are few and sporadic, usually with older age groups less likely to be working part-time compared to the youngest group for whites, Filipinos, and Vietnamese in 1980. For Vietnamese men in 1980, however, the middle age group is more likely to be working part-time than the youngest age group. It should be noted though that except for whites, age effects are practically nonexistent in 1990.

Interestingly, other than a slightly significant negative effect for the older immigrant group among white and Filipino men, migration status is not important in determining part-time employment among the men in the study. However, English language fluency is a consistent and significant predictor of part-time employment among Vietnamese men for both years. Vietnamese men fluent in English are less likely to be working part-time, suggesting better incorporation into the labor force. This finding supports previous studies (Chiswick 1991; Kossoudji 1988; McManus et al. 1983) that find language proficiency among non-native speakers as important in economic assimilation of immigrants.

Determinants of Working Poor Status

A higher incidence of working poor status is observed for men than for women. Given that men are seen as the primary earners in a family or household, this has a direct impact on the well-being of these men's families. Results of the working poor modeling are presented in Table 6.7.

Human capital effects on working poor status are mixed across ethnic groups. Self-employment is the only human capital variable that proved to be significant across all groups, and appears to be a more important determinant of working poverty in 1990 than in 1980. Education seems to have paid off for whites, by keeping them from being employed and in poverty, but only in 1980. Curiously, the effects of education are positive for the three other migrant groups. Why higher education translates to working poor status (compared to less educational attainment) is as yet unclear, especially when these significant effects are maintained in 1990. It is possible though that migrant status may be instrumental (at least for Filipinos and Vietnamese) in this result, with those having difficulty finding a job opting to take marginal ones. As expected, disability contributes to working poor status for all groups except Indians. The significance of self-employment in predicting working poor status for all groups, particularly in 1990, may be a response to a tight labor market in the 1980s and can be viewed as a coping strategy among those who were laid off or otherwise could not find a job.

Across all ethnic groups, household heads are less likely to be working in poverty. Signifying that household heads are more likely to be adequately employed, this result has positive implications for overall family well-being.

Consistent effects of industry across all ethnic groups are observed for the trade industry, where employees are more likely to be working in poverty than those who work in manufacturing. Other industry effects include a negative effect of service employment for Indians and Filipinos, but a positive effect of the same for whites. Public administration employment is less likely to translate into working poor status for Indians and Filipino men in 1980. What is evident from the industry effects is that working poor status is more characteristic of men employed in the trade industry than in manufacturing. Economic shifts may have something to do with this, with movement away from manufacturing and the rise of small businesses which are usually involved in trade. Needless to say, small businesses are the most volatile of enterprises

Table 6.7 Odds of male working poor status by ethnic group[a] (reference category in parentheses)

Variables	White 1980	White 1990	Indian 1980	Indian 1990	Filipino 1980	Filipino 1990	Vietnamese 1980	Vietnamese 1990
Human Capital								
HS grad+some coll (<HS)	0.76	1.13	1.16	1.57	1.16	1.55*	2.18**	1.86*
Coll grad+postcoll (<HS)	0.52**	1.03	1.49*	1.42	1.62**	2.41***	2.72***	2.20*
Disability	2.77***	2.03**	1.08	1.49	2.08*	2.61**	2.56**	1.52
Self-employed	2.77***	2.97***	1.26	1.95***	1.01	2.59***	1.17	2.89***
Family & Household								
Householder	0.36***	0.39***	1.97*	0.47***	0.23***	0.40***	0.62	0.39***
No. workers in HH	0.91	1.09	1.15	1.03	0.84**	1.02	0.81	0.97
Industry (Manufacturing)								
Agric/mining/const	1.27	1.38	0.64	0.79	0.58**	0.98	0.70	2.05*
Transp & communications	0.84	0.83	0.61	1.30	0.46**	1.05	0.98	0.61
Trade	1.40*	1.70**	1.25	1.92***	0.78	1.62**	1.27	2.66***
Business	0.90	0.61	0.95	0.64	0.75	0.69	0.67	3.00**
Service	1.46*	1.63**	0.41***	0.93	0.54***	1.09	0.94	1.36
Public administration	1.01	0.74	0.21*	0.51	0.34***	0.80	0.99	ni

Demographics								
31–45 yrs (16–30 yrs)	0.44***	0.46***	0.64*	0.83	0.82	1.08	0.91	0.83
46–64 yrs (16–30 yrs)	0.26***	0.25***	0.90	0.54**	0.56***	0.73*	0.82	0.57*
Migration & Language								
Migrated < = 10 yrs (nat)	1.45	1.36	0.79	1.45	1.51**	2.03***	0.52	0.49
Migrated 11+ yrs (nat)	1.07	1.09	0.36**	0.59	0.79	0.84	0.92	0.36*
Fluent in English	0.85	0.81	0.92	0.54*	0.98	0.61*	0.49***	1.00
Sample Selection Factor	0.66***	0.56***	0.71*	0.59***	0.58***	0.43***	0.43***	0.49***
Intercept	0.99	0.68	0.18**	0.98	2.22**	0.77	2.11	0.82
Likelihood Ratio X^2	6700.0	7747.6	5414.3	6328.0	10296.1	8569.7	2788.5	1068.9
Degrees of Freedom	12724	14444	9916	11224	17392	16844	5409	1651

[a] Models estimated using simultaneous multinomial logistic regression; models with missing variables (ni) with binary logistic regression.

and therefore may contribute to working poverty status. This rise in small businesses is also supported by the significance of the self-employment variables earlier.

Although not particularly consistent between 1980 and 1990, there is evidence that working poor status is more characteristic of the younger age group of men in the study. Significant age effects are found for all groups. Particularly strong age effects are observed for whites, where the two older age groups are less likely to be working in poverty than the youngest age group. The oldest age group (46–64) is found to be less likely to be in poverty while working full-time for all groups, particularly in 1990. This is consistent with the study of Gardner and Herz (1992) which found working poor status to be more predominant among the young. A tight labor market situation making entry-level jobs difficult to come by could have contributed to this situation.

Some interesting assimilation effects are observed, all in support of the hypotheses expressed earlier. Recent migrants are more likely to be disadvantaged as shown by the significant positive effect of recent migration on working poor status among Filipinos in 1980 and 1990. The assimilation theory predicts that incorporation into the labor market is facilitated with increased duration in the United States, and this is supported by the negative association between "older" migration and working poor status for Indians and Vietnamese. Finally, language effects in the expected direction are observed for the three migrant groups, with those fluent in the English language less likely to be working in poverty.

Determinants of Job Mismatch

Job mismatch is believed to be a dilemma of the highly educated and the migrant. It is therefore expected that job mismatch would figure significantly in the Asian underemployment modeling, given their high educational attainments. The models in Table 7.8 reveal the factors that significantly influence job mismatch for the Asian groups and the white reference group.

The overwhelming influence of education on job mismatch is unequivocal. Time trends reveal that mismatch is characteristic of men with at least a college degree in 1980, but that this group experiencing mismatch expanded to include high school graduates in 1990. Decidedly, the tight labor market situation, particularly for entry-level positions, has something to do with this trend. Entry-level jobs that are usually ignored or by-passed by highly educated men are now being occupied by these same people, leaving the high school graduates (who used to occupy these entry-level positions) to vie for still lower ranked jobs. Household headship is not characteristic of the mismatched group, implying that household heads are more likely to be adequately employed. At the same time, white and Filipino men who are experiencing job mismatch are less likely to be in households that have multiple workers.

Strong industry effects are observed for whites and Filipinos, with the highly negative relationship implying that mismatch among these two ethnic groups is most prevalent among those employed in manufacturing in 1980. For 1990, mismatch trends showed it to be more predominant among those employed in the trade industry (three out of four groups) and less predominant among those employed in service (all four groups), business (two of the four groups), public administration (two of the four groups), and in agriculture/mining/construction, when compared to manufacturing. In terms of generalizable industry trends, it appears that mismatch is most common among those employed in the trade industry and less likely among those in the service sector. A plausible explanation is that mismatch is not prevalent among the high occupational levels in the new economy industries like business and services where high-level jobs are managerial and supervisory. Instead, a greater likelihood of mismatch is found among employees of the manufacturing sector in 1980 and employees of the trade industry in 1990, where occupations may be of a more technical nature.

The Vietnamese reveal age and migration effects that are contrary to the experiences of the white, Indian, and Filipino men. While mismatch is mostly an experience of the younger age group among the three latter ethnic groups in 1980, middle-age Vietnamese men are the ones more likely to be mismatched. While migration status translates to a higher likelihood of mismatch among whites and Filipinos, native-born Vietnamese men are more apt to be mismatched. Differences in the age effects and the migration effects of mismatch reveal the differences in the educational backgrounds of the ethnic groups. While white, Indian, and Filipino migrants have high educational backgrounds that can land them high-level white-collar jobs, these same characteristics are more prevalent among the native-born Vietnamese. Vietnameses occupancy of high-level jobs may be more likely among older native-born men.

Gender Differences in Asian Underemployment

The underemployment models of both genders show some common trends but there remain distinctive gender differences in the determinants of the different underemployment categories. The succeeding

Table 6.8 Odds of male job mismatch by ethnic group[a] (reference category in parentheses)

Variables	White 1980	White 1990	Indian 1980	Indian 1990	Filipino 1980	Filipino 1990	Vietnamese 1980	Vietnamese 1990
Human Capital								
HS grad+some coll (<HS)	0.44***	9.68**	0.21***	1.71	1.08	5.31**	1.15	5.75**
Coll grad+postcoll (<HS)	4.26***	200.30***	3.86***	31.19***	3.25***	106.70**	17.12***	129.02***
Disability	0.84	1.13	0.80	1.43	1.14	0.82	1.22	0.85
Self-employed	1.15	1.00	0.52***	0.98	0.32***	0.50***	0.64	1.58
Family & Household								
Householder	0.27***	0.57***	0.83	1.17	0.44***	0.77***	1.16	0.63*
No. workers in HH	0.47***	0.91*	1.00	0.98	0.64***	0.97	1.00	0.90
Industry (Manufacturing)								
Agric/mining/const	0.47***	1.17	0.76	0.59**	0.16***	0.41***	0.39*	0.83
Transp & communications	0.61**	1.55*	0.82	1.08	0.28***	0.92	0.59	1.16
Trade	0.54***	2.39***	0.90	2.39***	0.27***	1.22	0.87	2.44***
Business	0.59***	0.51**	1.05	0.96	0.35***	0.36***	1.09	0.90
Service	0.33***	0.48***	0.25***	0.52***	0.20***	0.38***	0.40***	0.49***
Public administration	0.76	1.11	1.03	0.73	0.17***	0.48***	0.50	0.27**

Demographics							
31–45 yrs (16–30 yrs)	0.84	1.27	0.99	1.25	0.92	0.97	1.62*	1.97**
46–64 yrs (16–30 yrs)	0.49***	1.35	0.70**	1.28	0.79*	1.02	1.70	1.70
Migration & Language								
Migrated <= 10 yrs (nat)	2.22*	2.59*	1.02	1.58	2.48***	1.42*	0.30*	0.35
Migrated 11+ yrs (nat)	1.26	1.57	1.45	1.26	2.08***	0.99	0.66	0.25*
Fluent in English	1.03	0.76	3.82***	0.95	2.61***	1.17	1.46	1.23
Sample Selection Factor	1.05	1.02	1.03	1.12	1.31***	1.12	1.01	0.69
Intercept	1.55	0.01***	0.18**	0.01***	0.29***	0.01***	0.14*	0.04***
Likelihood Ratio X^2	6700.0	7747.6	5414.3	6328.0	10296.1	8569.7	2788.5	4338.32
Degrees of Freedom	12724	14444	9916	11224	17392	16844	5409	8737

[a] Models estimated using simultaneous multinomial logistic regression; models with missing variables (ni) with binary logistic regression.

discussion points out some generalizable, salient similarities and differences by gender.

The patterns in the influence of education are similar for men and women in the unemployment and job mismatch models. Women show positive education effects on part-time employment, particularly in 1990. However, the effects of education on men's part-time employment are few and mostly significant in 1980; by 1990, no education effects remain for men. It could be that this difference is through the earlier mentioned assumption of the stereotype of the man as the primary income earner, which has left part-time employment as a last recourse among men. For women, however, part-time employment is an option either for those who do so voluntarily for childrearing reasons, for economic reasons (inability to find a full-time job), or for fulfillment reasons (the husband can afford to support the family but the wife still wants to work). The influence of education also is different between men and women in the working poverty models. While education does not play a significant role in determining working poverty among women, education is an important predictor of working poverty in men, particularly among the migrant groups. In short, highly educated Indian, Filipino, and Vietnamese men are more likely to be among the working poor compared to less educated men. It is interesting to note that for whites, men's and women's models show that education pays off by keeping the whites with advanced degrees from being among the working poor. It is possible that the differential effect of education between whites and the three other groups reveals an immigrant coping strategy of taking whatever job is available. However, what explains the gender differences may be the primary income earner stereotype for men, or that immigrant women have been more successful in finding jobs than the men.

Disability is a strong predictor of unemployment, part-time employment, and working poor status for men and women. People with some form of limiting disability are incorporated into the labor market through marginal employment (underemployment in lower level jobs). The same conclusion can be maintained for self-employment, which is consistently positive and significant for the part-time and working poverty models, but negative in the job mismatch models. Some mismatch among the self-employed is observed among women, a trend that can be attributable to voluntary decision making.

Significant variation between men and women characterizes the influence of the family and household variables on underemployment. A strong negative relationship between household headship and worker composition in the household to unemployment and working poor status is observed for men and women. While scattered evidence is found for the influence of family and household variables on part-time employment, there is a strong negative influence of household headship on men's part-time employment. At the same time, while there is minimal influence of family and household variables on mismatch of women, household headship and worker composition in the household is again a strong predictor of male mismatch. What the results suggest is that for men, household headship ensures a distinct effort to strive for adequate employment, given that being a male household head is negatively related to an increased likelihood of being underemployed. The results for women are not as strong and consistent.

More gender commonalities are observed with the industry variables. Industry effects also show that unemployment is less likely in the service and business sectors for women, and more likely in agriculture/ mining/construction and trade for men. Part-time employment is predominant in the agriculture/mining/construction, trade, and service sectors for men and women. Working poverty also is consistently more likely in the trade sector for men and women. Employment in the trade sector increases the likelihood of mismatch for both genders, while employment in the service sector decreases mismatch. In general, it appears that important industrial sectors that consistently determine underemployment relative to the manufacturing sector are the trade and the service sectors. Employment in trade has figured in every category of underemployment for men and all but one (unemployment) underemployment category for women. At the same time, employment in the service industry has worked to decrease underemployment in general, except for increasing the likelihood of part-time work.

Women reflect more age differences in underemployment than men. Age is negatively related to unemployment and working poverty for women, while it is so only for the male working poverty models. On the other hand, older women are generally more likely to be employed part-time and mismatched, while the opposite is true for men. It is believed that the cultural expectations of primary breadwinner, childrearing, and sex roles figure into the explanation for these gender differences in age effects.

Migration and language effects are strongest in the working poverty and mismatch models, with patterns consistent between genders. However, while migration still is a significant predictor of part-time employment and unemployment in women, negligible migration effects on the two underemployment models are observed for men. Again, the need for immediate incorporation of men into the labor force (regardless of type of work) may explain this trend, while women have the option to wait for a good job, be employed part-time, or have lesser employment options (other than unemployment and part-time work) open to them.

The results of the underemployment models of the eight groups discussed reveal the different backgrounds that influence the employment outcomes of different groups. Human capital characteristics, family and household situations, industry incorporation, demographic, and migration variables all differentially impact on the different ethnic and gender groups. In some situations, time differences are also apparent. This study documents support for migrant disadvantage hypotheses, by showing strong positive migration status effects (except for female part-time work) on underemployment.

7

The Underemployment of Asian Workers: Concluding Thoughts

This study assesses the economic assimilation of Asians in the United States. Specifically, it goes beyond determining whether they have a job or not by evaluating the adequacy of their employment. I measure the incidence of unemployment, part-time employment, full-time employment with low pay, and job mismatch to give a better picture of the employment situation of Asians in the United States.

In general, the results show support for past research on majority-minority employment experiences. The minority groups experienced an increased prevalence of underemployment compared to whites. At the same time, minority groups revealed an increased likelihood for the economic forms of underemployment, despite controls for such critical factors as education and family situations. Significant is the effect of migrant status, particularly recent immigration experience on the likelihood of underemployment for the minority groups, except the Vietnamese. The expected disadvantage of family situations for female employment was not supported in this study.

Summary of Major Findings

In Chapter 1, the basic research questions for this study were identified. Based on the analyses in the preceding chapters, a synthesis of the results as they address the research questions can now be presented.

Question 1. How predominant is the experience of underemployment among Asians in the United States? How different are the specific Asian underemployment experiences from those of whites and of the other Asian groups in the study?

Underemployment is widespread among Asians in the United States, with the proportion underemployed in 1980 ranging from 50 percent for Indians to 41 percent for Vietnamese, compared to 36 percent for whites. In 1990, total underemployment had a minimal decline, but was still substantial for the Asian groups with the proportion underemployed ranging from 47 percent for Indians and 35 percent for Vietnamese compared to 35 percent for whites.

Assessing the distribution of ethnic groups by underemployment types, the results reveal that most of the underemployed whites are working part-time, followed by job mismatch, working poor, and unemployed. A majority of the underemployed Indians and Filipinos are experiencing job mismatch, followed by part-time employment, working poor, and unemployed. The Vietnamese underemployed are predominantly working poor, followed by part-time employed, unemployed, and mismatched.

Question 2. *What are the determinants of the different forms of underemployment for each group and how do these determinants vary across groups?*

Education increases unemployment among Indian and Filipino women while decreasing the same for white and Vietnamese women. It also increases unemployment among Filipino and Vietnamese men in 1980. By 1990, except for whites, education has no effect on men's unemployment. Education plays a significant role in increasing the likelihood of part-time employment for women and minorities, but decreases the same for white men. Weak education effects on working poverty are observed for women, with education generally decreasing the likelihood of working in poverty among women (except the Vietnamese). However, minority men are found to have increasing likelihoods of working poverty status with increasing education, while the opposite effect is observed for white men. The most significant effects of education are found in the job mismatch models, with college graduates and those with advanced degrees from all groups, more likely to experience job mismatch.

The effects of disability status are generally positive for most groups in determining the economic forms of underemployment. Disability status has no effect on the likelihood of job mismatch. The same positive effects of self-employment are found in predicting part-time employment (except for the Vietnamese) and working poverty for all groups.

The effect of household head status on unemployment, part-time employment (except for Indian women and Vietnamese men), and working poverty (except for Vietnamese men) is consistently negative and significant for all of the groups studied. This effect is maintained in the job mismatch model for whites and Filipinos only. Similarly, the number of workers in the household has a negative impact on unemployment for all groups, but weak and mixed results for the rest of the underemployment categories. The presence of a young child in the household showed minimal effects on underemployment, with results generally inconsistent with expectations. It is negatively related to white female unemployment and Indian and Filipino female working poverty status. However, having a young child in the household increases the likelihood of job mismatch among Indian women.

Industrial sector effects mostly reveal the preponderance of unemployment among those in the manufacturing sector, as shown by the mostly significant negative relationship of the different industries to unemployment, particularly of women. Minimal industry effects are observed for men, except for white and Filipino men who show significant positive effects of employment in the agriculture/mining/construction and the trade sectors on unemployment. More industry effects on part-time employment are observed for women than men. The predominantly positive effects imply that part-time employment is less likely in the manufacturing sector.

Employment in the following four industries generally led to an increase in part-time employment for most groups: agriculture/mining/construction, trade, business, and service industries. Working poverty status is more likely among those employed in the trade (except Indian men and Vietnamese women) and service (except Indians and Filipino men) industries. It is also more likely among white and Filipino women employed in the agriculture/mining/construction industry. Employment in the service industry results in a decreased likelihood of job mismatch for all groups. Some evidence of increased likelihood of job mismatch is observed for those employed in trade (except Filipinos), and transportation and communication (except Vietnamese, Indian men, and white women). Job mismatch is most likely among Filipino men employed in the manufacturing sector.

The minimal age effects on unemployment show a decreased likelihood of unemployment among the older white and Filipino age groups compared to the younger age group. However, older Indians are more likely to be unemployed than younger ones. Age effects show the middle age group as more likely to be employed part-time for all women except Vietnamese women, and only for Vietnamese men. White men in the middle age group, however, are less likely than the youngest age group to be working part-time. On the other hand, the oldest age group of white and Filipino women, as well as white, Filipino, and Vietnamese men showed a decreased likelihood of part-time employment compared to the youngest age group. Across all ethnic and gender groups (except Vietnamese women), working poverty is observed to be less likely among the older age groups compared to the youngest age group (16–30 years old). Job mismatch is more likely among the older female age groups, but more likely among the youngest age group (except Vietnamese) for men.

Consistent with expectations, recent Indian female and Filipino male and female migrants are more likely to be unemployed than their native-born counterparts. At the same time, recent Indian and Filipino women migrants are less likely than their U.S.-born counterparts to be employed part-time. Working poverty is more likely among recent Indian and Filipino migrants, but this effect disappears with increased duration in the United States. Recent migration status increases the likelihood of job mismatch for all groups except Indian men and all Vietnamese.

Proficiency in the English language emerged as a significant negative predictor of unemployment for the minority groups. The same language effects are observed in predicting part-time employment for migrant women and Vietnamese men. English language proficiency is important in decreasing working poverty for all of the migrant groups. Minimal language effects are observed for women; however, Indian and Filipino men who are fluent in English are more likely to experience job mismatch.

Question 3.   To what extent does immigrant status affect the experience of underemployment?

The effects of immigrant status on underemployment vary by type of underemployment. These effects are more apparent for women than for men. Immigrant status significantly increases the likelihood of experiencing unemployment, working poverty, and job mismatch for Indian and Filipino women. It decreases the chances of part-time employment for immigrant Indian and Filipino women. Immigrant white women also experience increased chances of mismatch. On the other hand, immigrant Filipino men are more likely to experience unemployment, working poverty, and job mismatch than their native-born counterparts. However, older Indian and Vietnamese migrants are less likely to experience working poor status.

The most consistent assimilation predictor of underemployment appears to be English language fluency, which is significant in decreasing unemployment, part-time employment, and working poor status, and job mismatch among Indian, Filipino, and Vietnamese women, as well as unemployment, part-time employment, and working poor status among the same groups of men. English language proficiency increased the likelihood of mismatch among Indian and Filipino men.

Question 4. *Does underemployment show differential returns to human capital across Asian groups as was found in previous research on employment patterns? Are there gender differences in the influences of human capital on underemployment within and between groups?*

Yes. While the effects of education on the different types of underemployment are more or less consistent across groups, the most striking example of different returns to education is found in the negative influence of education on working poor status only for white men, while the effect is positive for the Asian men. At the same time, education decreases the chances of unemployment for white men and women, while it increases the same for the minority groups (except Vietnamese women).

Education appears to decrease the likelihood of unemployment for whites, but increases the likelihood of the same for Indian women, Filipinos, and Vietnamese men. On the other hand, increasing educational backgrounds increases the chances of part-time employment for women and minority groups, but decreases the same for white men. Weak or minimal education effects are observed for the women's groups. However, the results for white men show reduced chances of working poverty status with increasing education, while minority men reveal a greater likelihood for working in poverty. As expected, strong educational effects are observed in the job mismatch models, with college graduates and those with advanced degrees more likely to experience job mismatch. This is true for all ethnic groups and both genders.

Disability status increases the likelihood of unemployment, part-time employment, and working poor status for all groups (except Indian women for part-time employment, and Indian men and Vietnamese women for working poverty). However, disability status does not have an effect on job mismatch for all groups.

Self-employment has minimal effects on unemployment. However, it is more apt to increase part-time employment for all groups except the Vietnamese. Self-employment increases the likelihood of working in poverty for all groups. The effects of self-employment on job mismatch is seen mostly for women, where self-employment increases the likelihood of job mismatch for all women's groups except Indian women. Self-employed Indian and Filipino men are less likely to be mismatched.

Question 5.   *How do family considerations affect the underemployment experience of the Asian groups in this study? Is the influence of family and household variables the same between gender and within and between Asian groups?*

The effect of family and household considerations on underemployment is generally to decrease the likelihood of underemployment.

Household head status decreases the likelihood of all the types of underemployment. It decreases unemployment and working in poverty for all groups, decreases part-time work for all but Vietnamese men and Indian women, and decreases job mismatch for white and Filipino women and for all but Indian men. Household headship represents the responsibility of maintaining the family/household and as a result means that household heads are pressured to gain adequate employment. However, female household heads are expected to experience greater chances of working in poverty, a result that is not borne out by the data.

The presence of other workers in the household is expected to represent decreased pressure, particularly for women, to seek employment or full-time employment, especially in the presence of young children or the elderly who have to be cared for. The results show support for effects contrary to expectations. The number of workers in the household decreases the chances of unemployment for all groups but Filipino women, increases the likelihood of white and Indian female working poor status as well as that of male Filipinos, and increases the chances of job mismatch of Indian and Filipino women while decreasing the same for white and Filipino men.

The presence of a young child in the household, which was expected to have a positive impact on women's underemployment, showed very minimal effects. White women with young children have reduced chances of unemployment. Contrary to expectations, no effect of having a young child is apparent for determining part-time employment. Indian and Filipino women had decreased likelihoods of working poor status if they had a young child, while Indian women are more likely to be mismatched in the presence of a young child. Results of this variable in general show effects contrary to expectations. While child care is still a concern among parents, it appears that facilities are in place and are available to address this need. It does not appear to keep already working women from taking on inadequate jobs just to accommodate some compromise for child care. In short, the presence of a young child in the household does not increase the likelihood of underemployment for the women in the study.

Question 6. *Is there any difference in the underemployment experience of Asians in the United States between 1980 and 1990?*

Yes. Total underemployment between 1980 and 1990 declined for all Asian groups. Indians experienced decreases in unemployment and job mismatch, an increase in part-time employment, and the same levels of working poverty. Filipinos had the same levels of unemployment, a slightly lower percentage of part-time employment, lower working poverty and job mismatch. The Vietnamese had lower unemployment and working poverty rates in 1990, higher part-time employment, and similar levels of job mismatch.

Among the human capital variables, disability status appears to be more important in determining unemployment and part-time employment in 1990 than 1980. Given the bleak labor market situation, workers may have found it more difficult to find jobs after losing a job. Disability claims may have increased in the light of increased unemployment, as a way to provide or supplement income. At the same time, self-employment is more significant in predicting working poor status in 1990 than 1980. This adds support to the conjecture that self-employment may be an adaptive strategy in the absence of other adequate employment opportunities. The effects of education on underemployment is more or less consistent between 1980 and 1990. An exception is that graduation from high school and having some college education increased the likelihood of job mismatch in 1990 compared to a negative influence or no effect in 1980 for most groups. This finding points to the fact that job mismatch in 1990 affects high school graduates as well as those with some college education.

Minimal changes in the effects of family and household variables on underemployment are seen between 1980 and 1990, especially for men. Among those considered are the change from a negative to positive influence of number of workers in the household on the part-time employment of Indian women, the increased importance of household head status in decreasing the likelihood of working poor for women in 1990, the positive influence of number of workers in the household on job mismatch for whites and Indian women in 1990, and the negative influence of number of workers in the household on Asian men's unemployment in 1980.

The industrial determinants of underemployment between 1980 and 1990 show the emergence of the agriculture/mining/construction sector as an important determinant of part-time employment for men and women in 1990. At the same time, the trade sector appeared as an important predictor of part-time employment and working poor status for men in 1990. Service-sector employment also increased in importance in determining part-time employment of men in 1990.

Changes in age effects show middle-age women as more likely to be employed part-time in 1990, except for the Vietnamese. Older Filipino women are also more likely to be mismatched in 1990, compared to being less likely to be so in 1980. On the other hand, men in the oldest age group are less likely to be of working poor status in 1990 compared to 1980, but less likely to be mismatched in 1980 than in 1990.

Recent immigration and poor English language proficiency are important determinants of part-time employment for Indian and Filipino women in 1980. Recent migration effects in determining job mismatch are observed in 1990 for three of the four female groups. Poor English is important in determining working poor status of Indian and Filipino men in 1990, but more important in determining job mismatch for the same groups in 1980.

Underemployment Model Fit and Model Components

A total of sixteen underemployment models are tested, one for each gender-ethnic-year combination. Each model is comprised of five blocks of variables, which perform differently in determining the different types of underemployment.

Consistent with the findings of Lichter (1988), Clogg and Sullivan (1983), and Blau and Ferber (1992), minority groups are more likely to be underemployed than whites. In this case, each of the Asian groups had an equal or higher prevalence of underemployment across all underemployment categories, when compared to whites.

Human capital theory predicts general underemployment among those with greater education. The models partially supported this. Education lowers the possibility of the economic forms of underemployment, but increases job mismatch. Similar to the findings of Nelson (1988) and Chiswick (1983, 1986), whites revealed education effects on underemployment consistent with expectations. However, the negative effects of increased education on underemployment is not apparent in all underemployment categories for minority groups. Unexpected results such as increasing the likelihood of working in poverty among minority men and increasing the likelihood of part-time employment among women are also observed. These may be a function of the additional effects of minority status whereby education effects are affected by an interaction with immigrant status. At the same time, the predominance of service jobs characterized by part-time employment (Sheets et al. 1987) can explain the high incidence of part-time employment among women, since more women workers are found in the service sector. The effects of disability and self-employment are consistent with expectations.

   The detrimental effects of family and household situations on the underemployment, particularly of women, are not found in the models. The effects of the family and household variables are either weak or inconsistent with the hypotheses in general. Household head status did keep the workers from being underemployed, but female household headship did not reflect the anticipated positive relationship with under-employment as in Blau and Ferber (1992) and Sheets and colleagues (1987). A similar opposite result is observed for the presence of a young child in the household, which did not seem to keep women from getting adequate employment (except for the positive influence of CHILDHH in the job mismatch equation of Indian women). Despite the findings of Hayghe and Bianchi (1994), having a young child in the household de-creased the likelihood of underemployment for some groups of women. This could be because society has responded to the child care needs of families that wish to accommodate women's employment, by setting up institutional facilities to oversee the child care function. That day care these days is considered routine can attest to this. At the same time, the presence of a child may indicate greater need for resources, therefore necessitating adequate employment for extra income. Finally, the num-ber of workers in the household did not perform as consistently as ex-pected. Instead of serving as alternative sources of income that can po-tentially free women to stay at home or work part-time, the presence of other workers in the household seems to indicate the general work ethic of the members of the household (the general tendency to seek adequate employment). However, in a few cases, the number of workers in the household did encourage part-time work and working poverty among certain groups of women.

   The general industry effects on underemployment are consistent with expectations. The increased likelihood of part-time employment in the service and trade sector is reflective of the general characteristics of jobs in these sectors (Sheets et al., 1987). At the same time, that unemployment is less likely in these sectors attests to the fact that these are the emerging industries in the United States at present. Similarly, that job mismatch is less likely in these same sectors reflects the low educational backgrounds needed to fill the low-skill, low-wage jobs that characterize the positions in these sectors.

In general, younger workers are expected to experience greater underemployment than older workers (Clogg and Sullivan 1983; Hauser 1974; Sicherman 1991).This finding is supported by the results of this study. Only in a few instances like part-time employment and job mismatch are some of the older age groups more likely than the younger ones to experience underemployment. Being fresh out of school as well as the lack of work experience and skills can be responsible for the greater likelihood of underemployment among the young.

Assimilation effects on the employment particularly of the immigrant groups are consistent with expectations. The migrant disadvantage literature that documented the disadvantage of immigrants on earnings (O'Hare and Felt 1991; Wong and Hirschman 1983) and occupational status (Nelson 1988) can include underemployment as another economic assimilation experience affected by migrant status. Recent migrants have increased the likelihood of being unemployed, mismatched, and working poor. Consistent with the findings of Kossoudji (1988), English language proficiency is also a significant determinant of underemployment among Asians, with those proficient in English less likely to experience the economic forms of underemployment but more likely to endure job mismatch.

Implications of Underemployment Results on Minority Groups

Among the groups in this study, it is apparent that whites enjoyed the greatest degree of adequate employment when compared to all the minority groups except for Vietnamese women. In addition, whites are more likely to be working part-time, while the minority groups had higher incidences of working poverty and job mismatch. It appears, therefore, that complete economic assimilation among Asians is not yet existent, as evidenced by the more advantaged position of whites in the labor force.

The immigration of Indian professionals and students which started with the promotion of technical assistance in the 1940s between India and the United States (Minocha 1987) is reflected in the highly educated population base of Indians in the United States by 1980. This situation is translated in the high prevalence of job mismatch found among Indians (particularly for men), in fact the highest among the groups in this study. At the same time, migrant status disadvantage effects are the least among the Indians compared to the rest of the minority groups in the study, indicating that excessive human capital may in fact overcome some of the disadvantages of migrant status. In particular, it may reflect the high incidence of professional recruitment and student migrants mentioned by Minocha (1987).

Filipino underemployment reflects the myriad of ways by which they immigrated to the United States. Initially as nationals between 1898 and 1934 where there was no screening for skills (Cariño 1987), then as unskilled agricultural workers in the early 1900s (Melendy 1977), to a post-1965 wave of highly educated and skilled professionals as well as dependents of military servicemen (Cariño 1987), the different pathways by which Filipinos got into the United States are seen in their experiences of underemployment. The value for and pursuit of higher education appears to be a characteristic common in Filipinos and Indians, as reflected by a high prevalence of job mismatch among Filipinos. However, the availability of other ways to immigrate to the United States, particularly through family reunification, decreased the selective stock of Filipino immigrants with high human capital. This is most evident in the greater effect that that migrant status appears to have on Filipinos than those from either of the other two minority groups. This implies that Filipinos who arrived in the United States with legal status by means other than labor recruitment or education may initially have difficulty in landing a good job. However, their status improves with time, as evidenced by the lack of significance of the older migrant variable in some of the models.

A consistent determinant of underemployment for the Vietnamese is English language proficiency, indicative of the language problems that these refugees faced on coming to the United States. This same language barrier as well as their lower educational background may be keeping them from adequate employment (Gordon 1987). Unlike the Indians, and similar to the Filipinos but at an extremely higher incidence, the granting of legal status (through refugee status for the Vietnamese) by means other than the selective screening for occupational capabilities results in a population base of mixed skills, translating into different employment experiences including economic forms of underemployment. This is reflected in the lack of migrant status effects on underemployment observed for the Vietnamese since their refugee status allows them to seek employment freely in the United States and compete with nationals. Low educational backgrounds coupled with language difficulties have made it hard for the Vietnamese to adjust to the U.S. labor market. This is best reflected in high rates of economic underemployment, the minimal significance of the education variable for Vietnamese women (except in the job mismatch model), the increased likelihood of underemployment for Vietnamese men, and the significance of language proficiency for both groups of Vietnamese.

The effect of the 1965 Immigration Act which favors family reunification is basically to dilute the selective immigration of highly educated Indian and Filipino professionals. While occupational migrants are screened for their skills and productivity, favoring family reunification over occupational preferences in immigration meant less screening for potential labor market success. As a result, the highly selective pool of professionals making up the base of the U.S. Indian and Filipino populations was combined with those with lesser skills or education. However, the immigration of the highly educated from these groups continues, reinforcing the "overachiever" (Hirschman and Wong 1984) view of Asians in the United States.

The results therefore show some evidence of the influence of past migration history on the labor market assimilation of ethnic groups. Indians with their high educational backgrounds and high-level skills and Filipinos, with their similar educational system and familiarity with American culture, as well as their command of the English language, experience greater economic assimilation in the U.S. labor market with fewer economic forms of underemployment and greater proportions of job mismatch. On the other hand, the Vietnamese, even without limitations on their employment opportunities, find it difficult to become incorporated into adequate employment. This situation is attributed to their educational background and more importantly, their poor command of the English language. Policy recommendations would include job search information and assistance for new immigrants as well as English language training, particularly for the Vietnamese.

Implications of Underemployment Results on Gender

Gender differences in economic performance are usually attributed to the time a mother has to stay away from work for childbearing and childrearing (Becker 1981), and its accompanying complexities (less commitment to full-time work, concentration in "female" fields, and others). The results of this study provide partial support for these findings.

The highly documented disadvantage of female heads of household and households with young children (Blau and Ferber 1992) in the economic success of women is not supported in this study. It appears that similar to men, female household heads experience a lesser likelihood of underemployment. At the same time, there is no evidence that the presence of a young child in the household encourages underemployment among women (except for job mismatch of Asian women). The changes in the labor market appear to have made high labor force participation and the desire for adequate employment a fact of life for women. As a result, society in general and couples in particular have made adjustments to accommodate this fact, be it in the form of changing sex roles or institutional support for child care and the like.

Variation in the levels of education completed by gender also does not explain gender differences in underemployment. Unlike whites where differential returns to education are observed between men and women, Asians do not vary significantly by gender in the effects of completed education on underemployment. As observed in Chapter 5, Asian women are at par with their male counterparts (or, in the case of Filipinos, ahead of them) in the level of education completed and the effects of education impact the underemployment experience of men and women similarly.

Gender differences start to emerge when examining industrial sector effects on underemployment. While employment in the service and trade industries is significant for both genders, women are observed to have stronger effects of these industries on underemployment. At the same time, men exhibit more effects for traditionally male occupations like agriculture, mining, and construction. Contrary to what Burtless (1990) found, more women suffered from employment in the manufacturing sector than men.

The greatest gender differences are observed on the effects of assimilation variables on underemployment. While migrants in general are expected to be disadvantaged in the labor market, women migrants appear to experience more disadvantage than men who migrate. Assimilation effects for male migrant groups are found to be less compared to those of women. In particular, Indian women experience a greater likelihood of unemployment, working poverty, and job mismatch if they are recent immigrants, while no corresponding effect was found for men. That the aforementioned professional recruitment may be predominantly male and that the women are tied movers (Sandell 1977) may explain this situation. Filipinos, on the other hand, reflect similar effects of immigrant status on both genders, implying that the reasons for entry into the United States as well as the human capital potential of Filipinos are similar between genders.

Overall, there is less variation in the basic determinants of underemployment between gender than there is across ethnic groups. The expected "double disadvantage" of Asian women in the workforce is only partially supported by this research. While there do not appear to be differences in the effects of education, family and household, and age determinants of underemployment by gender for Asian groups, differences in the effects of migrant status on underemployment by gender are noted, particularly for Indians.

Study Limitations and
Recommendations for Further Research

This study used the original LUF categories (Hauser 1974) in assessing underemployment because of data limitations of the U.S. Bureau of the Census PUMS files. While an expanded LUF version has been proposed (Clogg et al. 1986), the finer distinctions in the underemployment categories cannot be evaluated using the PUMS data. The PUMS data are used in this study because they provide enough cases of Asians to undertake a national study of Asian underemployment. The increasing availability of data on Asians, particularly from the Current Population Survey, in future years will make possible the assessment of underemployment using the expanded labor utilization framework.

A general model of underemployment is not complete without considering structural determinants. The effect of the labor market itself in determining economic success has been documented in the literature (Tienda and Wilson 1992a). Structural factors such as the area unemployment rate, percentage of a labor market that is minority, percentage of jobs that are female, and the like are found to be important determinants of economic performance in the labor market. While data problems (faulty FIBS code data for the earlier version of the 1990 PUMS) did not permit testing labor market variables in this study, incorporating them with the individual-level data will provide critical additional explanations of the determinants of underemployment.

Finally, a panel study design also is an appropriate approach to study underemployment. It permits the assessment of changes in the economic or employment position of respondents. Since immigrant and minority workers are assumed to be temporarily disadvantaged in the labor market, a panel design would allow an evaluation of whether this disadvantage is temporary or if other labor force dynamics emerge that are concealed when dealing with cross-sectional data.

Bibliography

Aldrich, John H. and Forrest D. Nelson. 1984. *Linear Probability, Logit and Probit Models.* Sage University Papers. Quantitative Applications in the Social Sciences, 45. Beverly Hills, CA: Sage Publications.

Arnold, Fred, Urmil Minocha, and James T. Fawcett. 1987. "The Changing Face of Asian Immigration to the United States." In *Pacific Bridges, The New Immigration from Asia and the Pacific Islands*, edited by James T. Fawcett and Benjamin V. Cariño. New York: Center for Migration Studies in association with the East-West Population Institute, East-West Center, Honolulu, 105–52.

Becker, Gary S. 1962. "Investment in Human Capital: A Theoretical Analysis." *Journal of Political Economy* 70(5, Pt 2):9–49.

———. 1965. "Theory of the Allocation of Time." *The Economic Journal* 75:493–517.

———. 1981. *A Treatise on the Family.* Cambridge, MA: Harvard University Press.

Bellin, Seymour S. and S. M. Miller. 1990. "The Split Society." In *The Nature of Work: Sociological Perspectives*, edited by Kai Erikson and Steven Peter Vallas. New Haven, CT: Yale Univeristy Press, 173–91.

Berk, Richard A. 1983. "An Introduction to Sample Selection Bias in Sociological Data." *American Sociological Review.* 48:386–98.

Blau, David M. and Philip K. Robins. 1989. "Fertility, Employment, and Child-Care Costs." *Demography* 26:287–99.

Blau, Francine D. and Marianne A. Ferber. 1992. *The Economics of Women, Men, and Work.* 2d ed. Englewood Cliffs, NJ: Prentice-Hall.

Block, Fred L. and Larry Hirschorn. 1987. "New Productive Forces and the Contradictions of Contemporary Capitalism: A Postindustrial Perspective." In *Revising State Theory: Essays in Politics and Postindustrialization*, edited by Fred L. Block. Philadelphia: Temple University Press, 99–126.

Bluestone, Barry and Bennett Harrison. 1982. *The Deindustrialization of America, Plant Closings, Community Abandonment, and the Dismantling of Basic Industries.* New York: Basic Books.

Borjas, George J. 1986. "Immigrants, Minorities, and Labor Market Competition." National Bureau of Economic Research Working Paper no. 2028. Cambridge, MA: National Bureau of Economic Research.

Bouvier, Leon F. and Anthony J. Agresta. 1987. "The Future Asian Population of the United States." In *Pacific Bridges, The New Immigration from Asia and the Pacific Islands,* edited by James T. Fawcett and Benjamin V. Cariño. New York: Center for Migration Studies in association with the East-West Population Institute, East-West Center, Honolulu, 285–301.

Bouvier, Leon F. and Robert W. Gardner. 1986. "Immigration to the U.S.: The Unfinished Story." *Population Bulletin* 41(4).

Burtless, Gary. 1990. *A Future of Lousy Jobs? The Changing Structure of U.S. Wages.* Washington, DC: Brookings Institution.

Cariño, Benjamin V. 1987. "The Philippines and Southeast Asia: Historical Roots and Contemporary Linkages." In *Pacific Bridges, The New Immigration from Asia and the Pacific Islands,* edited by James T. Fawcett and Benjamin V. Cariño. New York: Center for Migration Studies in association with the East-West Population Institute, East-West Center, Honolulu, HI, 305–25.

Chiswick, Barry R. 1983. "An Analysis of the Earnings and Employment of Asian-American Men." *Journal of Labor Economics* 1:197–214.

———. 1986. "Is the New Immigration Less Skilled than the Old?" *Journal of Labor Economics* 4:168–92.

———. 1991. "Speaking, Reading, and Earnings among Low-Skilled Immigrants." *Journal of Labor Economics* 9:149–70.

Clogg, Clifford C. 1979. *Measuring Underemployment: Demographic Indicators for the United States.* Studies in Population. New York: Academic Press.

Clogg, Clifford C. and Edward S. Shihadeh. 1994. *Statistical Models for Ordinal Variables.* Advanced Quantitative Techniques in the Social Sciences, no. 4. Thousand Oaks, CA: Sage Publications.

Clogg, Clifford C. and James W. Shockey. 1984. "Mismatch between Occupation and Schooling: A Prevalence Measure, Recent Trends and Demographic Analysis." *Demography* 21:235–57.

Clogg, Clifford C. and Teresa A. Sullivan. 1983. "Labor Force Composition and Underemployment Trends, 1969–1980." *Social Indicators Research* 12:117–52.

Clogg, Clifford C., Theresa A. Sullivan, and Jan E. Mutchler. 1986. "Measuring Underemployment and Inequality in the Work Force." *Social Indicators Research* 18:375–93.

DaVanzo, Julie. 1981. "Microeconomic Approaches to Studying Migration Decisions." In *Migration Decision Making, Multidisciplinary Approaches to Microlevel Studies in Developed and Developing Countries,* edited by Gordon F. De Jong and Robert W. Gardner. Pergamon Policy Studies on International Development. New York: Pergamon Press, 90–129.

Edwards, Richard, 1979. *Contested Terrain: The Transformation of the Workplace in the Twentieth Century.* New York: Basic Books.

Etzioni, Amitai and Paul A. Jargowsky. 1990. "The False Choice between High-

Technology and Basic Industry." In *The Nature of Work: Sociological Perspectives*, edited by Kai Erickson and Steven Peter Vallas. New Haven, CT: Yale University Press, 304–18.

Freedman, Marcia. 1985. "Urban Labor Markets and Ethnicity: Segments and Shelters Reexamined." In *Urban Ethnicity in the United States: New Immigrants and Old Minorities*, edited by Lionel Maldonado and Joan Moore. Urban Affairs Annul Reviews, vol. 29. Beverly Hills, CA: Sage Publications in cooperation with Urban Research Center, University of Wisconsin-Milwaukee, 145–65.

Gardner, Jennifer M. and Diane E. Herz. 1992. "Working and Poor in 1990." *Monthly Labor Review* 116(12):20–28.

Gardner, Robert W., Bryant Robey, and Peter C. Smith. 1989. "Asian Americans: Growth, Change, and Diversity." *Population Bulletin* 40(4).

Gordon, Linda W. 1987. "Southeast Asian Refugee Migration to the United States." In *Pacific Bridges, The New Immigration from Asia and the Pacific Islands*, edited by James T. Fawcett and Benjamin V. Cariño. New York: Center for Migration Studies in association with the East-West Population Institute, East-West Center, Honolulu, 153–73.

Grubb, W. Norton and Robert H. Wilson. 1989. "Sources of Increasing Inequality in Wages and Salaries, 1960–80." *Monthly Labor Review* 112(4):3–13.

Hauser, Philip. 1974. "The Measurement of Labor Utilization." *Malayan Economic Review* 19(1):1–15.

Hayghe, Howard V. and Suzanne M. Bianchi. 1994. "Married Mothers' Work Patterns: The Job-Family Compromise." *Monthly Labor Review* 117(6):24–30.

Hirschman, Charles and Morrison G. Wong. 1984. "Socioeconmic Gains of Asian Americans, Blacks, and Hispanics: 1960–1976." *American Journal of Sociology* 90:584–607.

Holzer, Harry J. and Wayne Vroman. 1992. "Mismatches and the Urban Labor Market." In *Urban Labor Markets and Job Opportunity*, edited by George E. Peterson and Wayne Vroman. Washington, DC: The Urban Institute Press, 81–112.

Hornbeck, David W. and Lester M. Salamon. 1991. *Human Capital and America's Future, an Economic Strategy for the Nineties*, Baltimore: Johns Hopkins Univeristy Press.

Hosmer, David W. Jr. and Stanley Lemeshow. 1989. *Applied Logistic Regression*. Wiley Series in Probability and Mathematical Statistics. Applied Probablity and Statistics Section. New York: Wiley.

Jensen, Leif. 1991. "Secondary Earner Strategies and Family Poverty: Immigrant-Native Differentials, 1960–1980." *International Immigration Review* 25:113–39.

Jiobu, Robert Masao 1990. *Ethnicity and Inequality.* SUNY Series in Ethnicity and Race in American Life. Albany: State University of New York Press.

Kanter, Rosabeth M. 1990. "The New Work Force Meets the Changing Workplace." In *The Nature of Work: Sociological Perspectives,* edited by Kai Erickson and Steven Peter Vallas. New Haven, CT: Yale University Press, 279–303.

Klein, Bruce W. and Philip L . Rones. 1989. "A Profile of the Working Poor." *Monthly Labor Review* 112(10):3–13.

Klein, Deborah P. 1973. "Exploring the Adequacy of Employment." *Monthly Labor Review* 96(10):3–9.

Ko, Gilbert K. and Clifford C. Clogg. 1989. "Earnings Differentials between Chinese and Whites in 1980: Subgroup Variability and Evidence for Convergence." *Social Science Research* 18:249–70.

Kossoudji, Sherrie A. 1988. "English Language Ability and the Labor Market Opportunities of Hispanic and East Asian Immigrant Men." *Journal of Labor Economics* 6:205–28.

Lalonde, Robert John and Robert H. Topel. 1990. *The Assimilation of Immigrants in the U.S. Labor Market.* National Bureau of Economic Research Working Paper no. 3573. Cambridge, MA: National Bureau of Economic Research.

Lichter, Daniel T. 1988. "Racial Differences in Underemployment in American Cities." *American Journal of Sociology* 93:771–92.

McManus, Walter, William Gould, and Finis Welch. 1983. "Earnings of Hispanic Men: The Role of English Language Proficiency." *Journal of Labor Economics* 1:101–30.

Meisenheimer, Joseph R., II. 1992. "How Do Immigrants Fare in the U.S. Labor Market?" *Monthly Labor Review* 115(12):3–19.

Melendy, H. Brett. 1977. *Asians in America: Filipinos, Koreans, and East Indians.* Boston: Twayne.

Miller, Paul W. 1992. "The Earnings of Asian Male Immigrants in the Canadian Labor Market." *International Migration Review* 26:1222–47.

Minocha, Urmil. 1987. "South Asian Immigrants: Trends and Impacts on the Sending and ReceivingCountries." In *Pacific Bridges, The New Immigration from Asia and the Pacific Islands,* edited by James T. Fawcett and Benjamin V. Cariño. New York: Center for Migration Studies in association with the East-West Population Institute, East-West Center, Honolulu, 347–73.

Nelson, Gloria Luz M. 1988. "Assimilation in the United States: Occupational Attainment of Asian Americans, 1980." PSTC Working Paper Series 88-03.

Providence, RI: Population Studies and Training Center, Brown Univeristy.

Noyelle, Thierry J. 1987. *Beyond Industrial Dualism, Market and Job Segmentation in the New Economy*. Boulder, CO: Westview Press.

O'Hare, William P. and Judy C. Felt. 1991. *Asian Americans: America's Fastest Growing Minority Group*. Population Trends and Public Policy no. 19. Washington, DC: Population Reference Bureau.

Pido, Antonio J. A. 1986. *The Philipinos in America: Macro/Micro Dimensions of Immigration and Integration*. New York: Center for Migration Studies.

Piore, Michael J. 1979. *Birds of Passage: Migrant Labor and Industrial Societies*. New York: Cambridge University Press.

Portes, Alejandro. 1981. "Modes of Structural Incorporation and Present Theories of Labor Immigration." In *Global Trends in Migration*, edited by Mary M. Kritz, Charles B. Kelly, and Silvano M. Tomasi. Theory and Research on International Population Movements. Staten Island, NY: Center for Migration Studies, 279–97.

Presser, Harriet. 1986. "Shift Work among American Women and Child Care." *Journal of Marriage and the Family* 48:551–63.

————. 1989. "Can We Make Time for Children? The Economy, Work Schedules, and Child Care." *Demography* 26:523–43.

Reskin, Barbara and Irene Padavic. 1994. *Women and Men at Work*. Sociology for a New Century. Thousand Oaks, CA: Pine Forge Press.

Rutledge, Paul James. 1992. *The Vietnamese Experience in America*. Bloomington: Indiana University Press.

Salamon, Lester M. 1991. "Why Human Capital? Why Now?" In *Human Capital and America's Future, an Economic Strategy for the Nineties*, edited by David W. Hornbeck and Lester M. Salamon. Baltimore: Johns Hopkins Univeristy Press, 1–39.

Sandell, Steven. 1977. "Women and the Economics of Family Migration." *Review of Economics and Statistics* 59:406–14.

Sheets, Robert G., Stephen Nord, and John J. Phelps. 1987. *The Impact of Service Industries on Underemployment in Metropolitan Economies*. Lexington, MA: Lexington Books.

Shihadeh, Edward and Clifford C. Clogg. 1989. "1980 Job Mismatch Cutoff." Manuscript. Department of Sociology, Louisiana State University, Baton Rouge.

Shin, Eui Hang and Kyung-Sup Chang. 1988. "Peripherization of Immigrant Professionals: Korean Physicians in the United States." *International Migration Review* 22:609–26.

Sicherman, Nachum. 1991. "'Overeducation' in the Labor Market." *Journal of Labor Economics* 9:101–22.

Siegel, Martha S. and Laurence A. Canter. 1990. *The Insider's Guide to the New U.S. Immigration Act of 1990.* Tucson, AZ: Sheridan Chandler.

Sjaastad, Larry A. 1962. "The Costs and Returns to Migration." *Journal of Political Economy* 70(5, Pt 2):80–93.

Spring, William. 1971. "Underemployment: The Measure We Refuse to Take." *New Generation* 53(1):20–25.

Sullivan, Teresa A. 1978. *Marginal Workers, Marginal Jobs: The Underutilization of American Workers.* Austin: The University of Texas Press.

Tang, Joyce, 1993. "The Career Attainment of Caucasian and Asian Engineers." *The Sociological Quarterly* 34:467–96.

Tienda, Marta and Ding-Tzann Lii. 1987. "Minority Concentration and Earnings Inequality: Blacks, Hispanics, and Asians Compared." *American Journal of Sociology* 93:141–65.

Tienda, Marta and Franklin D. Wilson. 1992a. "Migration and the Earnings of Hispanic Men." *American Sociological Review* 57:661–78 .

___. 1992b. "Migration, Ethnicity, and Labor Force Activity." In *Immigration, Trade, and the Labor Market*, edited by John M. Abowd and Richard B. Freeman. Chicago: University of Chicago Press, 135–63.

Tipps, Havens C. and Henry A. Gordon. 1985. "Inequality at Work: Race, Sex, and Underemployment." *Social Indicators Research* 16:35–49.

United States. House of Representatives. Committee on the Judiciary. 1980. *Immigration and Nationality Act, with Ammendments and Notes on Related Laws. Committee Print for the Use of the Committee on the Judiciary, House of Representatives, United States.* 7th ed. Rev. through Sept. 1, 1980. Washington, DC: U.S. Government Printing Office.

___. 1986. *The "Immigration Reform and Control Act of 1986" (P.L. 99-603): A Summary and Explanation. Committee on the Judiciary, House of Representatives, Ninety-Ninth Congress, Second Session.* Washington, DC: U.S. Government Printing Office.

United States. Immigration and Naturalization Service. 1980. *Statistical Yearbook of the Immigration and Naturalization Service, 1979.* Washington, DC: Immigration and Naturalization Service, Department of Justice.

———. 1986. *Statistical Yearbook of the Immigration and Naturalization Service, 1985.* Washington, DC: Immigration and Naturalization Service, Department of Justice.

———. 1988.*Statistical Yearbook of the Immigration and Naturalization Service, 1987.* Washington, DC: Immigration and Naturalization Service, Department of Justice.

———. 1991a. *An Immigrant Nation: United States Regulation of Immigration, 1798–1991.* [Washington, DC?]: Immigration and Naturalization Service, Department of Justice.

———. 1991b. *Statistical Yearbook of the Immigration and Naturalization Service, 1990.* Washington, DC: Immigration and Naturalization Service, Department of Justice.

United States. Office of Federal Statistical Policy and Standards. 1990. *Index: Standard Occupational Classification Manual.* Washington, DC: Office of Federal Statistical Policy and Standards, U.S. Dept. of Commerce.

Wilkie, Jane Riblett. 1991. "The Decline in Men's Labor Force Participation and Income and the Changing Structure of Family Economic Support." *Journal of Marriage and the Family* 53:111–22.

Winship, Christopher and Richard B. Mare. 1992. "Models for Sample Selection Bias." *Annual Review of Sociology* 18:327–50.

Wong, Morrison G. and Charles Hirschman. 1983. "Labor Force Participation and Socioeconomic Attainment of Asian-American Women." *Sociological Perspectives* 26:423–46.

Xenos, Peter S., Robert W. Gardner, Herbert R. Barringer, and Michael J. Levin. 1987. "Asian Americans: Growth and Change in the 1970s." In *Pacific Bridges, The New Immigration from Asia and the Pacific Islands*, edited by James T. Fawcett and Benjamin V. Cariño. New York: Center for Migration Studies in association with the East-West Population Institute, East-West Center, Honolulu, 249–84.

Index